BEHIND BARS: GENERAL CONVENTIONS

Behind Bars

GENERAL CONVENTIONS

Elaine Gould

This edition first published in 2023 by Faber Music Ltd
Adapted from *Behind Bars* (2011)
Brownlow Yard, 12 Roger Street, London WC1N 2JU
Typeset by Agnesi Text
Music examples engraved by Richard Emsley
Cover design by Dominic Brookman
Printed and bound in England by Caligraving Ltd

All rights reserved
© Elaine Gould, 2011

The right of Elaine Gould to be identified as author of this work
has been asserted in accordance with Section 77
of the Copyright, Designs and Patents Act 1988

A CIP record for this book
is available from the British Library

ISBN 0–571–54284–0
ISBN 978–0–571–54284–0

Complete edition of *Behind Bars* (0–571–51456–1) is also available

Published in German as *Hals über Kopf*
by Edition Peters and Faber Music Ltd (2014)

*To my mother and brother
and to my many composer friends
for their boundless enthusiasm and encouragement*

Foreword to the complete edition

Elaine Gould, in this wonderful monster volume, has written the equivalent of the Grove Dictionary for Notation. It is an extraordinary achievement, and if used by the next generation of composers and copyists will be a blessing for hard-working and long-suffering performers everywhere! Every chapter presents solutions and rules that will make our life easier, save rehearsal time and frustration, and will ultimately lead to better performances. What is important for a musician is to be able to spend rehearsal time on the music itself, without the hindrance of trying to decipher it. The clarity Elaine asks for is not a matter of dry rules or customs: it is part of the living texture of the music itself. I not only welcome her book unreservedly, but I would also pray that it becomes a kind of Holy Writ for notation in this coming century. Certainly nobody could have done it better, and it will be a reference for musicians for decades to come.

Sir Simon Rattle

Contents

Introduction xi

1 *Ground Rules* 3
2 *Chords – Dotted Notes – Ties* 45
3 *Accidentals and Key Signatures* 75
4 *Dynamics and Articulation* 99
5 *Grace Notes, Arpeggiated Chords, Trills, Glissandos and Vibrato* 123
6 *Metre* 149
7 *Tuplets* 191
8 *Repeat Signs* 217

Appendix 241
Further Reading 245
Copyright Acknowledgements 247
Index 249

Introduction

In an age where computers can do it all for us, what need is there for expertise in, or even a working knowledge of, the principles of notation?

Many will believe that given a certain level of expertise, computer processing enables the user to produce music of the highest quality. Software will make layout and spacing decisions, and produce a beautifully sharp and precise page of music. The innovation of computer technology is indeed essential since most performers today prefer or expect computer-generated material even if some professionals still say that well-spaced hand copying, or a composer's manuscript, tell us more about the music than the impersonality of a computer-set page ever can.

But computer-generated music must satisfy best practices if it is to fulfil its function. I hope that a thorough understanding of the principles set out in this book will complement the armoury of skills, shortcuts and techniques that the modern musician sitting at a computer has to hand. Computer software can take us so far; only the dexterity and subtlety of the human mind can make the ultimate informed choices notation frequently demands. The information presented in this book should therefore be relevant regardless of whether the user is sitting at a computer or undertaking the painstaking job of hand copying a manuscript. A computer programme will apply notation principles, but the operator must decide if these are the most apt solutions, and a trained eye is required to refine the settings and evaluate if the contents of the stave and the spacing on the page are really the most appropriate.

As musicians, we tend not to spend much time analysing why this or that piece of music looks good or bad, but there's no doubting that we can feel when something is not quite right, even if we don't know why. Musicians deserve the very best that the language of notation can provide, and the most elegant layout that can be achieved; in this way they will be free to give their all in performance. Through a mutual understanding of the rules and conventions of notation, the composer can 'speak' effectively to the performer, who then has the best chance of achieving a faithful interpretation of the composer's intentions.

It goes without saying that many of the views and practices expressed in *Behind Bars: General Conventions* are subjective. My own views regarding best practice are based on four decades of working with music notation, composers and performers, and I have attempted to present a clear, user-friendly guide. Any errors are my own.

It is my hope that the principles set out in *Behind Bars: General Conventions* will serve music for many years to come and that musicians can be safe in the knowledge that they will understand each other.

Historical context

The early twenty-first century is an appropriate time to re-establish principles of good practice that have governed notation over the last 150 or so years. New compositional techniques of the mid-twentieth century stimulated notational experiment and innovation, and that left a diverse legacy. The intention of *Behind Bars* is to encourage the use of established conventions where appropriate since what is familiar is of most help to the musician. The familiar can be read and understood quickly. There are often already so many different ways of notating the same thing that the invention of novel notation to give a score a particular uniqueness is unhelpful and potentially alienating. Unfamiliar notation takes much longer to assimilate; furthermore, the more complicated the notation, the greater the possibility is that it will create a barrier to the reader.

Skills of traditional engraving used to be passed down in publishing houses. In a post-engraving era, I have formulated conventions from analysis of historical engraving practices, consulting a cross-section of scores engraved over the last hundred years, as well as scores by known experienced engravers. In present-day classical publishing, the editions of Henle and Bärenreiter are notable models of good practice.

Behind Bars: General Conventions is in no way a history of music notation, but is a practical guide to present-day users who need to communicate their music accurately and effectively.

Using *Behind Bars: General Conventions*

Within the covers of this book, a clear, detailed hierarchy of headings should enable the reader to navigate the book easily and find information quickly. Related subjects are grouped together where practical; subjects that are treated elsewhere in different contexts are cross-referenced. In general, a topic is structured: definition – design – placing – use. Where practical, topics are handled as logical progressions from the elementary to the complex, and definitions are given where terminology is uncommon or potentially confusing. Foreign-language technical terms are used where they are in common usage in the English-speaking world, and such terms are presented in the text in italic – even though they may appear in roman type in a musical context. A basic knowledge of music theory is assumed.

Every facet of a piece of music, from placing symbols on and around the stave to choosing the most appropriate time signatures and repetition formats, is very much dependent on individual context. I have illustrated as many contexts as possible, and introduce comparative examples to train the eye to distinguish good practice from bad. There is no implied comment on musical merit in the choice of examples, nor in terms of the inclusion or exclusion of particular composers' works. References to scores in the text are likewise chosen simply for their notational attributes.

The mainstay of *Behind Bars: General Conventions* is to examine the complex set of rules on which good notation is founded. Effective communication results from establishing a convention and adopting a consistent approach. Where appropriate I have presented the rationale for certain conventions and rules, to make such conventions more memorable. My aim is to raise awareness of the many subtle and complex issues to be considered, and provide the tools to address them.

Elaine Gould
January 2011, revised October 2022

General Conventions

1
Ground Rules

CONTENTS

The stave 5

Clefs 5

Noteheads 9

Stems 13

Tails 15

Beams 17

Ledger lines 26

Octave signs 28

Using ledger lines or octave signs 32

Rest symbols 34

Barlines 38

Rhythmic spacing 39

Spacing symbols 41

The stave

The five-line stave

The size of every notational symbol is measured in proportion to the stave size. A stave-space is the distance between two stave-lines and is used as a measurement for notational symbols and spacing in this book.

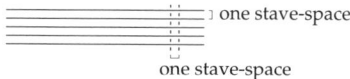

A piece of music should have a consistent stave size throughout. It is essential to choose a stave size that the player, singer or conductor is able to read comfortably.

The single-line stave

USES

- to notate instruments of indefinite pitch
- to notate sounds of indefinite pitch (e.g. percussive sounds) produced on pitched instruments
- to notate vocal sounds of non-specific pitch
- to notate a cue line of rhythm
- as an option to show approximate pitch

Clefs

Clef position

There are four clefs in common use. It is important to place each on the stave so that it centres precisely on the relevant stave-line.

The treble (or G) clef winds around the G line; the bass (or F) clef winds around the F line, and its dots fall each side of the F line:

C CLEFS

These centre on whichever line is to be designated as middle C. The five clefs are:

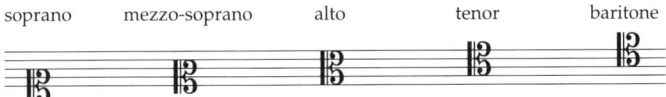

The C clefs in common use are the alto and tenor clefs. The alto clef centres on the middle stave-line. It covers the height of the stave. The tenor clef centres on the second stave-line down. It is the same height as the alto clef (the height of the stave), but placed one stave-line higher:

The other C clefs are used to replicate the original clefs of early music vocal scores.

PERCUSSION CLEFS

The following clefs are placed in the middle two stave-spaces to indicate that the stave contains notes of indefinite pitch:

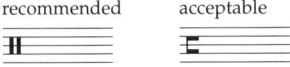

The clef is optional for a stave of fewer than five lines, since such staves are assumed not to signify pitches anyway. If used, place the clef as follows:

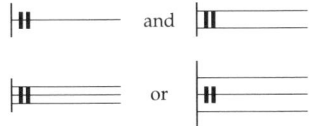

INDENTATION

A clef is indented into the stave by one stave-space (⌒) or a little less:

Clefs to use

Except for percussion, each stave must begin with a clef. Never omit the clef; only in hand-copied theatre and entertainment music has it ever been an accepted convention to use a clef on the first line and no other.

USING ALTO AND TENOR CLEFS

Among common orchestral instruments, only the viola uses the alto clef. The alto clef should be used for alto trombone parts.

Bassoon, trombone, cello, and occasionally double bass, use the tenor clef. Some nineteenth-century editions place tenor-voice parts in the tenor rather than the treble clef.

Changing clef

A change of clef placed after the beginning of the system is two-thirds of the size of the clef at the beginning of the stave (see following examples).

For performance material, stay in one clef for as long as is practicable, using up to at least three ledger lines rather than changing clef frequently. This shows the contour of the pitches, which a change of clef would obscure:

The practice of retaining the most commonly used clef at the beginning of the stave while inserting a new clef after it is obsolete. This includes the very start of a piece:

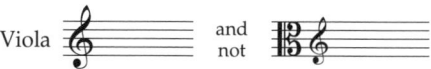

AT THE BEGINNING OF THE SYSTEM

Give warning of the clef change by placing the new clef at the end of the previous system before the barline:

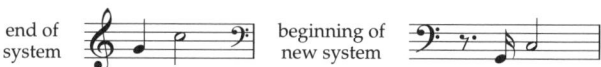

AT THE BEGINNING OF A BAR

The clef always goes before the barline, whether or not rests precede the entry:

The only clefs that appear directly after a barline are new clefs required for cues in instrumental parts, and clef changes after repeat sections (see *Changes after a repeat*, p. 235).

MID-BAR

Place the new clef between beats, rather than in the middle of a beat. This is least disruptive to the spacing of the bar:

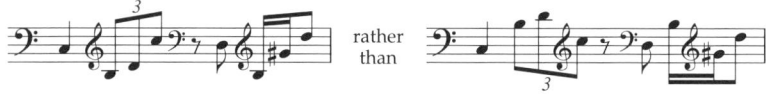

Between beats, change the clef after rests:

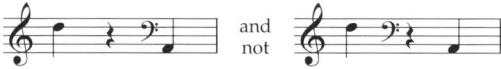

Should a new clef be unavoidable in the middle of a beat, position it between half-beats or another subdivision:

(For spacing with clef changes, see *Additional clefs and accidentals*, p. 43.)

BETWEEN PHRASES

In a passage of continuous playing, place a new clef between phrases, wherever this occurs in the bar. This placing overrules the above considerations. It enables the reader to see the pitch contour of the phrase intact. The clef separates two phrases rather than two bars or two beats:

WITH TIED NOTES

Avoid changing a clef during a tied note, as the tie will look cumbersome. If this cannot be avoided, the clef is best changed at a system break:

AFTER PERIODS OF RESTS

Where an instrument rests for more than a system, it is usual to return it to its commonest clef (provided this is suitable for the following entry). For example, a viola previously playing in the treble clef changes back to the alto clef. (This helps when reading a full score: the staves of some instruments can be immediately identified by their clefs.) Place the clef change at the end of the system after the player has finished: this is the least disruptive position as regards spacing. It is better than an immediate clef change before rests, which draws unwanted attention to the new clef at an arbitrary point:

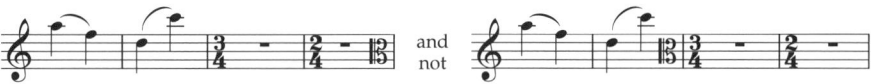

Where there needs to be a change from the more standard clef, retain this clef until the barline before the next entry. This placing alerts the performer to the change at the relevant point (i.e. at the entry), and not further back before a group of rests, where it may be overlooked:

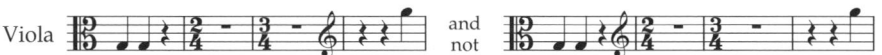

Noteheads

Shape and size

BLACK NOTEHEADS

These are oval-shaped and placed on the stave with a diagonal slant away from the stem:

WHITE NOTEHEADS

The minim: the notehead is oval-shaped with diagonal shading. It is usually slightly larger than the black notehead:

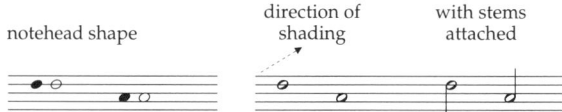

The semibreve: the oval notehead has greater width (in proportion 2½ semibreves to 3 black noteheads) and does not slant diagonally. Its shading slants slightly but in the reverse direction from the minim – a semibreve is not a stemless minim. White notes tend to be read by their shape, rather than by the presence (or not) of a stem, whereas with black notes the eye looks for a tail or beam – the correct shape for the notehead is therefore important:

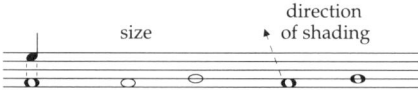

The breve: this can be notated in one of three ways:

Placing

The height of a stave-space determines the size of all noteheads, which is crucial to ease of reading. Noteheads too small in proportion to the stave make the music uncomfortable to read:

NOTES IN A SPACE

The notehead fills the space, touching the stave-line on each side of it, but without extending beyond either line:

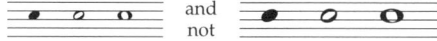

NOTES ON A LINE

The notehead is precisely centred on the stave-line. The unshaded centre of a white note must be visible when the stave-line runs through the notehead.

If the stave-lines are too thick and the noteheads too small, the centre of white notes may fill in with reproduction.

Diamond-shaped noteheads

The diamond shape has concave sides and is shaded on the diagonals as in the example below. When the notehead is in a space the top and bottom corners slightly extend beyond the stave-lines on either side. This is to give the notehead sufficient size to distinguish it from a minim. Diamond noteheads look small compared with the white oval:

A stem joins the diamond at the side of the notehead, and not at the central point (although the latter are used to replicate the notation of early music editions):

USES

- as harmonics in instrumental writing (except piano)
- as silently depressed keys in piano music
- to differentiate notes of unconventional technique in wind music
- to indicate singing through a wind instrument
- to indicate multiphonics
- as unvoiced sounds in vocal writing
- as an option for falsetto

Harmonic noteheads for bowed string instruments and woodwind remain white, regardless of duration. Harmonic noteheads for guitar are white or black according to duration.

Crossed noteheads

The cross comprises two unshaded diagonal lines. It fills a stave-space:

The double-sharp sign x is sometimes used for crossed noteheads, but is best reserved for use as an accidental symbol.

The stem joins the cross at the edge of the symbol, and not at its centre:

MINIMS AND SEMIBREVES

The unshaded area inside a white notehead is too small to add a cross without obscuring the white space. Instead, the cross is surrounded by a thin unshaded circle (the same shape for both minim and semibreve durations). In simple percussion writing, the crossed notehead is sometimes replaced with a diamond-shaped notehead, to make the durations slightly easier to read:

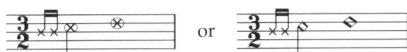

However, it is not recommended that crossed and diamond notes are mixed in this way.

USES

- in both instrumental and vocal writing, to notate percussive sounds and sounds of indefinite pitch on a five-line stave
- in percussion writing, to distinguish certain instruments or their beating spots, and to notate finger damping
- to distinguish spoken text
- in vocal music, to indicate styles between speech and singing
- as an option to show approximate pitch

Triangular noteheads

The triangular notehead denotes the highest/lowest possible pitch, where such a pitch cannot be specified.

The notehead may be black or white according to duration. It is a little larger than a minim notehead. The stem is attached to the centre of the base of the triangle. For a semibreve duration, two tied minims are clearer than a stemless notehead (see following example).

Place the notehead outside the stave, the exact distance from the stave depending on context:

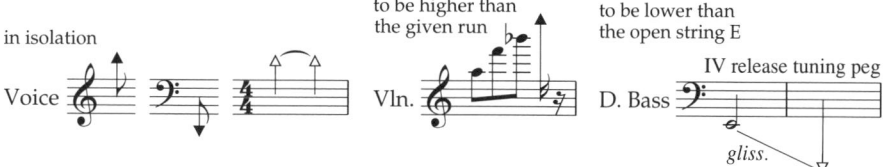

Do not use the triangular notehead for a pitch that can be defined. For example, the bottom note of a stringed instrument should be notated at its proper pitch, and a triangular notehead used only if the string is to be detuned to an unspecified pitch. If this is the case, an instruction must say so, as in the double bass example above.

(See also *Glissandos: To and from unspecified pitches*, p. 142.)

Stems

Stems should be thinner than the stave-line, but not so thin as to reproduce too faintly.

Stem direction

Notes above the centre stave-line take down-stems, notes below the centre stave-line take up-stems:

NOTES ON THE CENTRE STAVE-LINE

When notes are on the centre stave-line, the stems may go in either direction. The direction is determined by context. Continue the stem direction of surrounding stems that are in one direction only:

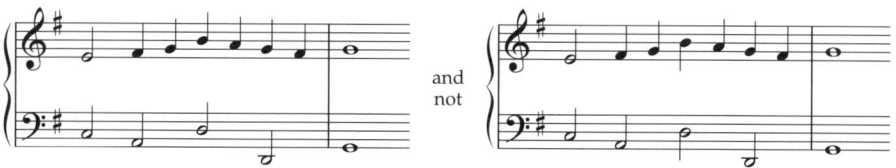

When the stem direction varies within a bar, maintain the stem direction of the notes that are part of the same beat or half-bar:

When there is no clear-cut case for either direction, the convention is to use a down-stem. Some editions use down-stems exclusively.

Some editions of vocal music use up-stems only, to allow the text to be placed close to the stave.

(See also *Stem direction on beamed groups*, p. 24; for single-stemmed chords, see *Stem direction*, p. 47; for *Double-stemmed writing*, see p. 52.)

Stem length

The standard length of a stem is one octave (i.e. 3½ stave-spaces) from the centre of the notehead:

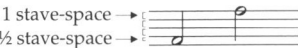

(For grace notes, see *Design*, p. 125.)

NOTES ON LEDGER LINES

Stems for notes on more than one ledger line extend to the middle stave-line (marked ∗ below):

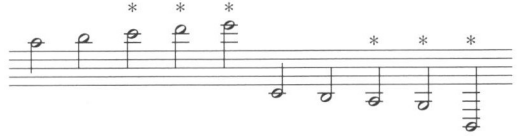

DOUBLE-STEMMED WRITING

As stems fall further outside the stave, they are progressively shortened. The shortest stem length is a sixth (2½ stave-spaces): no stem should ever be shorter than this.

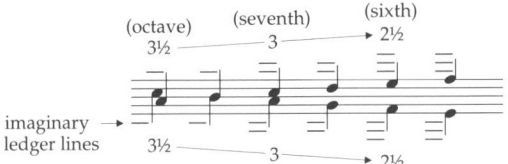

stem length measured by (interval) and in stave-spaces

CHORDS

Stem length is measured from the note closest to the open end of the stem. This stem is the length it would be as a single note.

Stems within the stave are one octave long (3½ stave-spaces); stems for notes on ledger lines reach to the middle line:

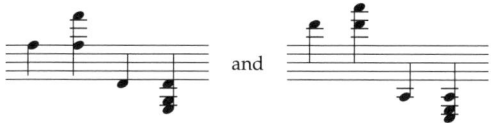

Stems outside the stave are progressively shortened (as in *Double-stemmed writing*, opposite):

ADDING TAILS AND BEAMS

The standard stem length allows room for one or two tails or beams to be attached. In double-stemmed writing, the stem length of 2½ spaces accommodates only one tail or beam. For each additional tail or beam, the stem must be lengthened (see *Additional tails*, p. 16; also, *Additional beams*, p. 19).

Tails

Quaver tails

The engraved design of tail is 2½–3¼ stave-spaces long (3–3¼ is the norm). This ensures that the tail of an up-stemmed note finishes opposite or just above the notehead:

tail length 2½   3   3¼

The tail of a down-stemmed note may curve as far as to touch the notehead:

When a stem is shorter than 3 stave-spaces, the tail should avoid overshooting the notehead. A stem length of 2½ spaces can accommodate a tail of this length, but the stem should be lengthened for a longer tail:

Semiquaver tails

The semiquaver tail fits inside the quaver tail. The tails are a little less than a stave-space apart. Usually the combined length of the semiquaver tails is ¼–½ stave-space longer than the quaver tail. Sometimes stems are slightly lengthened for this, although they most commonly remain the same length:

Additional tails

These are added further from the notehead than the quaver tail. Extend the length of the stem for these:

So that tails do not touch the noteheads of down-stemmed notes, some editions shorten the tails while others lengthen the stems.

Notes on ledger lines

The outer stave-line must be clearly visible; tails closer to noteheads will obscure ledger lines:

Beams

(For beaming notes into groups to reflect the time signature, see *Beaming according to the metre*, p. 153.)

Design

Beam thickness is ½ stave-space. The distance between beams is ¼ stave-space. Thus the correct placing of three beams is:

All stems should pass through all inner beams to the outer beam, not just the outside stems of the group, as in some (mostly French) editions:

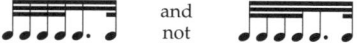

FRACTIONAL BEAMS

These inner beams are the length of a notehead:

(For *Fractional beams*, see p. 157.)

Beam placing within the stave

A horizontal beam should not be placed in the middle of a space. The closeness of beams and stave-lines is uncomfortable to read and there is a danger that the narrow white spaces will disappear at a small stave size and with poor reproduction, so that both beams and stave-lines are obscured:

A beam must be attached to the top or bottom of a stave-line or else be centred on the line. The only possible exception is the placing of four beams within the stave (see p. 18).

Angled beams should have all beams attached to a stave-line at both ends of the beamed groups (see *Angled beams within the stave*, p. 20).

The following rules will avoid placing beams in the middle of a stave-space.

TWO BEAMS

Up-stems: the outer beam hangs from or centres on the stave-line.
Down-stems: the outer beam sits or centres on the stave-line.

These positions are fixed so that when an inner beam (the semiquaver beam) is added, it does not end up in the middle of a space:

THREE BEAMS

Up-stems: the outer beam hangs from the stave-line.
Down-stems: the outer beam sits on the stave-line.

Any other outer beam position results in a beam ending up in the middle of a space (marked →):

FOUR BEAMS

If possible, place the beams slightly further apart than normal, so that each is attached to a stave-line:

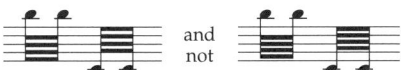

Where there is no the facility to alter the distance between beams, this will result in a beam in a stave-space. This compromise is acceptable as long as the reproduced image is sufficiently high quality that the spaces either side of the beam do not fill in.

Beam placing affecting stem length

ONE AND TWO BEAMS

A stem may be slightly lengthened or shortened to allow for correct beam positioning within the stave (as described above). The stem length (including the width of the outer beam) should be as close to 3½ spaces (normal stem length) as possible.

When notes are in a space, the stem length is 3½ spaces:

When notes are on a line, the stem is shortened to 3¼ spaces:

stem length   3½   3¼   3¼   3½   3¼   3¼

This prevents the inner beam from being incorrectly placed when it is added:

incorrect

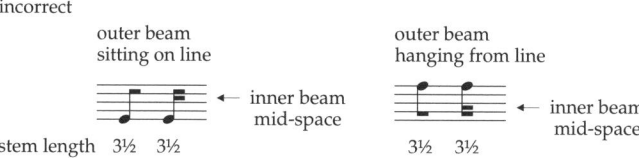

ADDITIONAL BEAMS

The outer beam moves further away from the notehead to allow space for additional beams. Beams should never be closer to the notehead than the correct position of the semiquaver beam (2½ spaces). Extend stems for the additional beams:

NOTES ON LEDGER LINES

There must be one clear stave-line between the innermost beam and the first ledger line:

Angled beams

DEGREE OF BEAM ANGLE

The angle of beams gives individual character to a page of printed music. Different music setters may use slightly different angles.

Beam angles should not deviate far from the horizontal because the eye perceives duration on the horizontal plane. Usually, they cross no more than one stave-line. Thus the wider the interval, the more flattened the beam angle becomes in relation to the size of the interval:

Avoid steep angles through stave-lines, as these create an uncomfortable visual lattice effect:

Slight angles through stave-spaces should be avoided (see *Angled beam within the stave*, below).

A long group of notes may have a beam that crosses one or possibly two stave-spaces:

To avoid creating a steep beam angle the beam of shorter groups should not cross more than one stave-space:

Notes spaced very close together horizontally (closer than three spaces) take only a slight angle (¼ or ½ space) regardless of the interval:

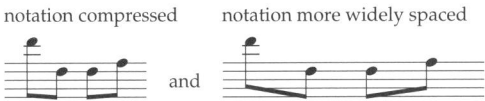

ANGLED BEAMS WITHIN THE STAVE

Both ends of a slanted beam should be attached to a stave-line. This is the engraving tradition: no beam starts or finishes in the middle of a stave-space, since the white space between stave-line and beam results a thin wedge that is likely to 'fill in' at a small stave size or with poor reproduction or print resolution:

Adding a second and third beam: the correct placing of the quaver beam ensures that neither end of a semiquaver beam is in the middle of a space (see *Beam placing within the stave*, p. 17).

With the addition of a third beam, the beams must slant a whole stave-space (a). Any other angle will result in one of the beams beginning or ending in the middle of a stave-space (b), which is less than satisfactory.

In the past, to ensure both ends of all beams are attached to stave-lines, some editions have slightly widened the distance between beams to allow for an angle of less than a stave-space (c). This is a good compromise:

(For a detailed study of beam angles, see Ted Ross, *The Art of Music Engraving and Processing*.)

ANGLED BEAMS MODIFYING STEM LENGTH

The stem that is going to be the shorter determines the starting point of the beam (marked ↓ below). This stem may be shortened to 3 stave-spaces (a seventh) when inside the stave and to 2½ stave-spaces (a sixth) when outside the stave. The wider the interval the longer the other stem(s) must become to join the beam:

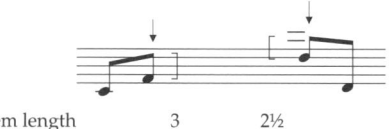

NOTES ON LEDGER LINES

When all the notes of a beam fall outside the first ledger line, the beam takes only a slight slope, regardless of the pitches. Intervals of a second take a slope of ¼ stave-space; all wider intervals take a slope of ½ stave-space:

BEAMS OUTSIDE THE STAVE

Some editions have steeper angles outside the staves since there is no need to take account of crossing stave-lines. However, matching angles look better:

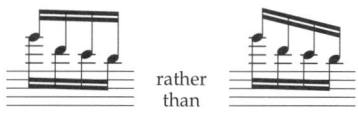

Direction of beam angle

The beam is angled in the direction of the interval for a pair of notes or the outside interval for a group of notes.

MULTI-DIRECTIONAL BEAMED GROUP

The outer notes of the group determine the beam direction:

This is regardless of the direction of the majority of the notes:

(But see also groups of concave shape, below.)

The beam angle reflects the interval between the outside notes, and not the angle of the group's most extreme interval:

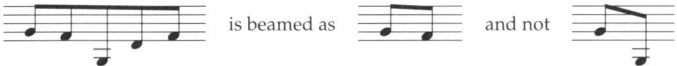 is beamed as 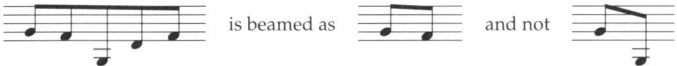 and not

The beam is horizontal when:

(a) the group begins and ends with the same note:

(b) there is a repeated pattern of pitches:

(c) an inner note (marked ↓ or ↑) is closer to the beam than either of the outer notes. Such a group forms a concave shape:

A group of convex shape takes a sloping beam:

A group with both shapes takes a horizontal beam since there is an inner note (↓ or ↑) that is closer to the beam than one of the outer notes:

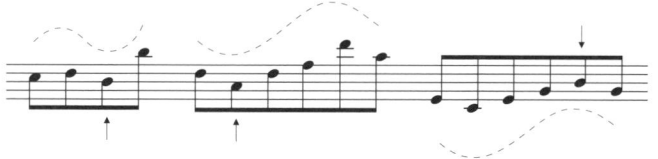

TWO PITCHES ONLY IN A GROUP OF THREE OR MORE NOTES

Where there is only one different note at the beginning or end of the group and this note is furthest away from the beam, the beam is horizontal:

When this single note is closest to the beam, the beam slopes:

Where there is an equal number of each note, the beam may slope:

Alternatively, these beams may remain horizontal (this can look better in repeated figuration).

CLEF CHANGE WITHIN A BEAMED GROUP

The beam slants according to the position of notes on the stave, regardless of a clef change. Lengthen a stem so that a beam does not run through the new clef:

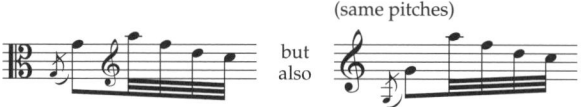

CHORDS

The note closest to the beam determines the beam angle:

Stem direction on beamed groups

In order to beam together notes that would alone take different stem directions, one or more notes takes stems in the 'wrong' direction.

EQUAL NUMBERS OF NOTES EITHER SIDE OF THE MIDDLE LINE

The note furthest from the centre of the stave (marked ↓ or ↑) dictates the stem direction:

UNEQUAL NUMBERS OF NOTES ON EITHER SIDE OF THE MIDDLE LINE

The majority of stems go in the 'correct' direction:

The exception is when a minority of notes are much further from the middle stave-line than the majority. In this case it is better to have a majority of shorter stems in the 'wrong' direction, rather than many long stems:

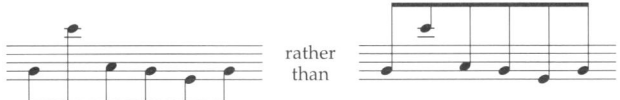

GROUPS WITH NOTES EQUIDISTANT FROM THE MIDDLE LINE

For a two-note group, either stem direction is valid:

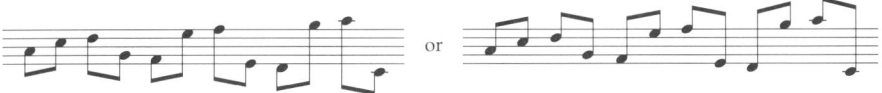

The same is true when equal numbers of notes are equidistant from the middle line:

The context may determine the direction. For example, notes adjacent to the group in question may take stems in one particular direction:

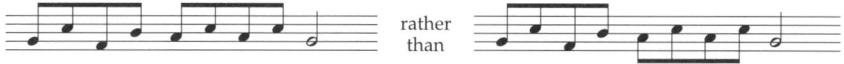

Where there is no obvious case for either direction, it is the convention to use down-stems. Editions that use down-stems exclusively for middle-line notes use down-stems for all groups with notes equidistant from the middle line as well.

VISUAL CONSIDERATIONS

When groups within a passage together roughly span the width of the stave, visual considerations may suggest maintaining the same stem direction for the whole passage. In the following example, this allows all slurs and harmonic indications to remain next to their noteheads:

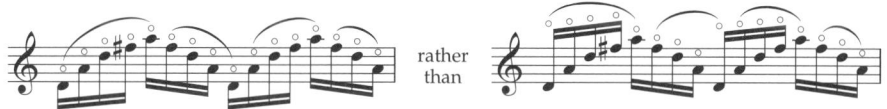

Dividing beams for wide intervals

Groups with wide intervals take up a disproportionate amount of vertical space outside the stave. Such groups are sometimes divided so as to contain the stems within the stave. This is visually unhelpful as the grouping of beats is confused:

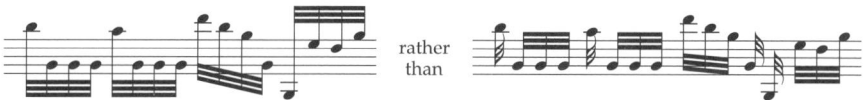

(See also *Beams with opposite stem directions*, p. 26.)

Beams with opposite stem directions

Very wide intervals may take a beam centred between the stems in order to save vertical space and long stems. This is provided that no stem is shorter than a sixth (2½ spaces) and that the top and bottom stave-lines remain clear of a beam:

Where the outside notes are at a different pitch, slope the beam in the direction of the outside interval, since a slanted beam is more conspicuous against stave-lines than a horizontal one:

This same principle is used for combining groups of notes shared between two (or even three) staves in braced parts (keyboard and harp). Stems point towards a beam centred between the two staves (see last example, p. 73).

Ledger lines

Ledger lines are an extension of the stave. They are spaced the same distance apart as stave-lines, but they are about twice as thick.

It is important that ledger lines are visibly thicker than stave-lines so that a player reading a passage of ledger-line notes can take in the number of ledger lines at a glance.

The ledger line extends slightly beyond either side of the notehead and is just over two spaces long (a). Ledger lines of adjacent notes should not join up (c); the lines may be slightly shortened in cramped conditions (b):

Grace notes take ledger lines that are shorter and thinner than full-sized notes, in proportion to their smaller noteheads:

(See *Grace notes: Design*, p. 125.)

ADJACENT-NOTE CHORDS

Ledger lines extend beyond the noteheads on both sides of a stem, between the stave and the outermost pair of adjacent notes.

When the displaced note (marked ↓ or ↑) is on a line, the ledger line extends the full width of both notes; when the displaced note is in a space, the last ledger line is shortened to single notehead width:

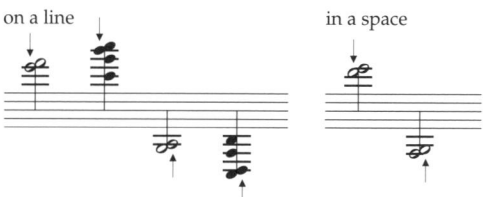

Notes further from the stem end than the adjacent pair take single-width ledger lines:

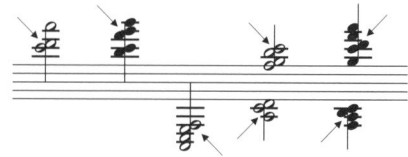

(For notation of *Adjacent-note chords*, see p. 48.)

DOUBLE-STEMMED ADJACENT NOTES AND OVERLAPPING PARTS

The two parts may share ledger lines, which should extend either side of all noteheads between the stave and the displaced part.

When parts overlap, ledger lines that are not shared by the part whose pitch is closest to the stave should not cut through its stem:

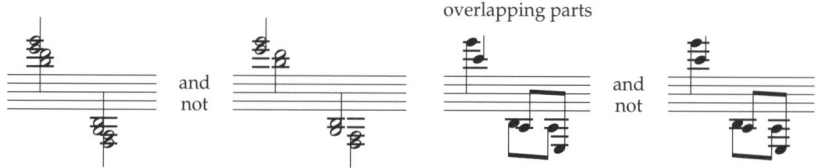

(See also *Double-stemmed writing: Overlapping parts*, p. 53.)

Octave signs

The octave sign is written in italic, the numeral '8' is 1½ stave-spaces high. The optional 'va' is placed flush with the top of *ottava sopra* (*8va*), flush with the base of *ottava bassa* (*8va*).

		raise pitch	lower pitch
ONE OCTAVE	in Italian	*ottava sopra* or *ottava alta*	*ottava bassa*
	notated	*8*⁻⁷ or *8va*⁻⁷	*8*₋₁ or *8va*₋₁ or *8va bassa*₋₁ or *8ba*₋₁
TWO OCTAVES*	notated	*15*⁻⁷ or *15ma*⁻⁷	*15*₋₁ or *15ma*₋₁
THREE OCTAVES	notated	*22*⁻⁷ or *22ma*⁻⁷	*22*₋₁ or *22ma*₋₁

* French editions use *16*⁻⁷

Placing

Place the numeral just left of the first note to which it applies:

If a note or chord has accidentals, the numeral may be placed flush with the extreme left accidental rather than aligned with the notehead. However, the exact placing often depends on the available space. When space is tight, the numeral may be placed directly above or below the note.

The extension line

Indicate the extent of the transposition with a line of dashes (hereafter called a dotted line). The line extends from the top edge of the *8* for *8 sopra* and the base of the *8* for *8 bassa*, and runs parallel to the stave.

Usually the octave sign will be outside all other notation. It must never cut through other symbols, as this is visually confusing. If restricted vertical space does not permit the dotted line to be parallel with the stave, it can be lowered or raised to follow the contour of the notes, in order not to collide with other notation:

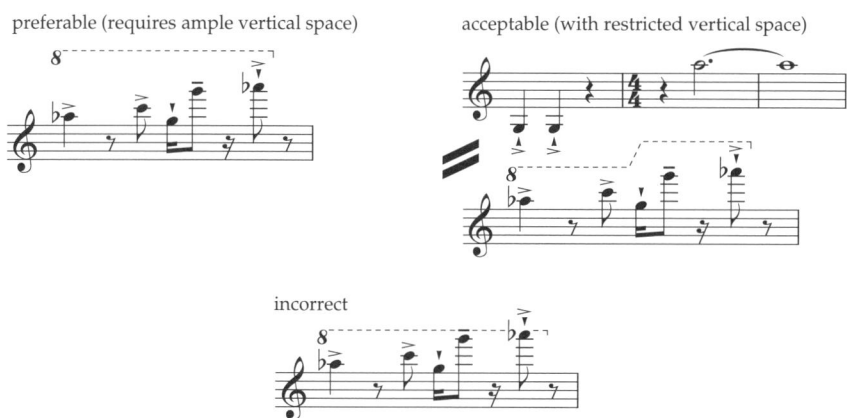

However, avoid deviation from the horizontal if at all possible.

When there are phrase marks or tuplet brackets as well as octave signs, whichever covers the longest duration goes on the outside:

FOR A WHOLE SYSTEM

Place an extension line for a whole system outside all other notation (notes, short slurs, articulation and dynamics), since the dotted line visually cuts off all information outside it. In addition, once the line is established, the player does not need to keep referring to it, and therefore information that potentially changes (e.g. dynamics) is better placed closer to the stave.

Only tempo markings and piano pedal indications remain outside an octave extension line that continues for a whole system.

GROUND RULES

ACROSS A SYSTEM BREAK

End of a system: extend the dotted line as far as the last barline (and not beyond it).

Beginning of a system: place the 8 (optionally in brackets) just before or flush with the first note:

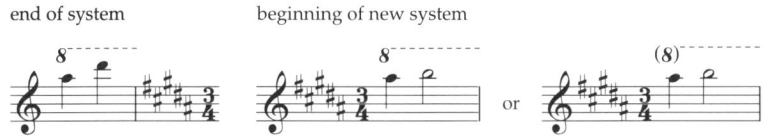

Length of the extension line

Terminate the octave transposition with a corner ⌐ (rather than just a vertical stroke, as this is less visible). Place this immediately after the last notehead(s), including duration dots:

Although the practice of some editions, avoid terminating the line at the end of the duration:

However, the line extends for the written duration of the note when a trill is notated with a wavy line and in repeated bars when the following abbreviation is used:

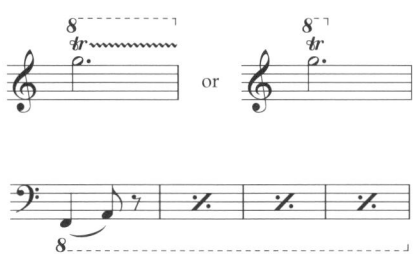

(For *Repeated bars*, see p. 231.)

When material to be repeated is notated inside repeat marks, the extension line continues only for the length of the notated material, not for the length of the repeat:

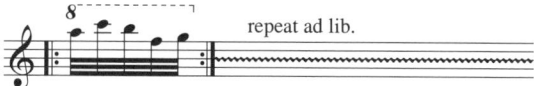

EXTENSION LINE ACROSS RESTS

Continue an extension line across short rests rather than using separate octave signs:

When rests are more extensive, the notes between them take separate octave signs:

Octave sign for single notes

It is advisable to use an end corner after the *8*, so that it is absolutely clear that only the single note is affected:

Vertical extension line

When the octave indication is some distance above or below the first or final note to which it refers, extend a vertical dotted line to the notehead, for clarity:

Clefs indicating notes to sound at a different octave

The clefs 𝄞 𝄢 may be used in a full score to indicate that instruments such as the piccolo and double bass are written respectively an octave lower and higher than sounding.

Do not use these clefs to replace genuine octave transpositions (Britten used them in his late scores, especially for piano and harp). The clefs tend to go unnoticed, as the player is unaccustomed to reading them.

'With the octave'

The Italian term *coll'ottava* written *col 8(va)* or *con 8(va)* is a shorthand for writing octaves in keyboard music. The indication is followed by a dotted line for its duration.

Placed above the stave, the indication means *col 8va sopra*: 'with the octave above the written pitch'. Placed below the stave, the indication means *col 8va bassa*: 'with the octave below the written pitch'.

If there is room, it is always better to write out the octave pitches. However, to do so in a passage such as the following would take up a lot more space:

Using ledger lines or octave signs

Use up to at least three ledger lines before transposing pitches up or down an octave and using an octave sign.

Never use an octave sign when an instrument could move into a higher-pitched or lower-pitched clef:

Music for woodwind and strings can use up to five ledger lines before moving into an octave transposition. Octave transpositions are unhelpful, as a player identifies a written pitch with a given fingering. The fingering does not duplicate the other octave, as it does on a keyboard.

Brass instruments and voices should never need octave signs.

Keyboard and harp music may make more extensive use of octave signs than other instruments (see example *More extensive use of octave signs*, p. 34).

In performance material, always use ledger lines in preference to octave signs for isolated notes or chords. Even in piano music it is more helpful to show the contour of the music in order to alert the player to the necessary leap of the hand. Players can easily read at least four ledger lines at a glance.

A full score that is not used to play from may replace ledger lines with the octave or even the two-octave sign as necessary, to save space between staves:

These octave signs should not be transferred to a playing part, except where absolutely necessary:

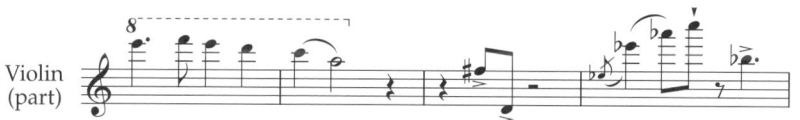

Using octave signs

A written change of octave tends to obscure the contour of a line and so, wherever possible, keep a phrase intact at the chosen octave. Change octave between phrases. Where this is not possible, change octaves between beats or half-beats; an octave change in the wrong place (⌐⌐) obscures the relationship between the intervals:

Even when a passage makes more extensive use of octave signs, the pitches of each figure should be preserved at the same octave, so that the intervallic leaps are clearly visible:

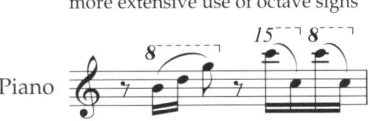

Using *loco*

The octave transposition is cancelled by *loco* (Italian, 'in place'), which should be used after an extended passage of octave transposition. It is also used when the same written (or a neighbouring) pitch is immediately repeated after the octave transposition, and as a reminder after a rest (where it may take brackets):

It need not be used where frequent alternation of *ottava* and *loco* pitches would be cluttered by *loco* indications, or where a significant pitch difference renders it unnecessary:

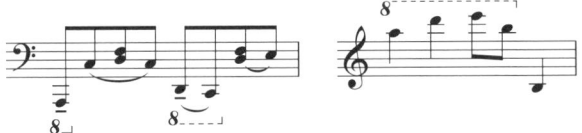

(For octave signs affecting accidentals, see *Octave changes*, p. 79.)

Rest symbols

Design

BREVE, SEMIBREVE AND MINIM RESTS

These rests are the length of a minim notehead. The semibreve and minim rests are ½ stave-space thick. The semibreve hangs from the second line down; the minim rest sits on the centre stave-line:

The breve rest occupies a whole stave space and is the same length or, more commonly, half the length of the semibreve and minim rests:

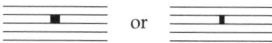

CROTCHET REST

The rest starts in the top stave-space and finishes in the bottom space. The bottom hook cuts through the second stave-line from the bottom:

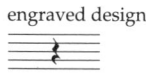

QUAVER AND SHORTER RESTS

The quaver rest sits above the middle stave-line and extends down to the second stave-line from the bottom:

Shorter rests are placed so that each hook is in a separate stave-space. The 𝄾 occupies the middle two spaces, the 𝄿 the top three spaces, the 𝅀 all four spaces:

(For rest alignment with another part, see *Horizontal position of rests*, p. 159.)

Vertical placing of rests within the stave

Rests remain centred within the stave regardless of the pitches of surrounding notes:

The rest moves up or down within the stave when a beam joins notes across a rest and in double-stemmed writing (see pp. 36–7). From the centre of the stave, rests move an exact number of stave-spaces up or down, so that they remain correctly positioned in relation to the stave-lines:

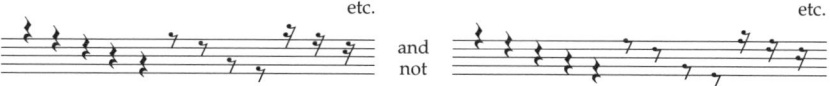

BEAMS ACROSS RESTS

Place the beam in its normal position. If necessary, rests may move away from the centre of the stave to a position closer to surrounding notes, in order to avoid colliding with a beam. It is better to reposition rests than to have them in the middle of the stave, as this forces surrounding stems to be very long (and therefore indication of rhythm becomes too far from the notes):

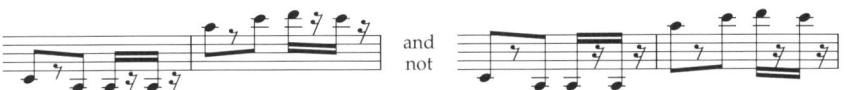

(See also *Beaming across rests*, p. 164.)

Placing rests in double-stemmed writing

Two parts on a stave with different durations require their own sets of rests.

A rest moves further from the centre of the stave or to outside the stave should parts otherwise collide.

RESTS WITHIN THE STAVE

For clarity, upper-part rests are usually placed above the centre stave-line, lower-part rests below the centre line:

When one part lies outside the stave (on ledger lines), crotchet, quaver, and shorter-value rests for the other part may move back to the centre of the stave:

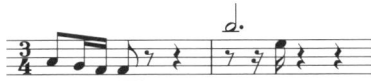

Semibreve and minim rests must never stray across the centre stave-line:

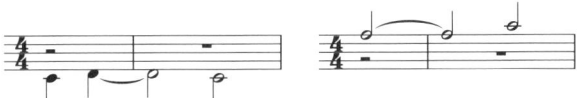

When both parts have rests simultaneously, as in strict contrapuntal writing, separate these with at least one stave-line:

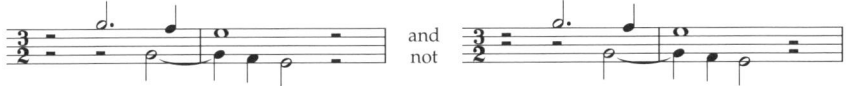

Many editions place all minim and semibreve rests on only the outside stave-lines, to avoid confusion; some avoid rests on the middle stave-line, for the same reason (see 4/4 example below).

Except in strict contrapuntal writing, two separately stemmed parts on a stave with the same durations share a rest wherever possible.

RESTS OUTSIDE THE STAVE

Minim and semibreve rests are placed on a ledger line. The ledger line moves far enough away from the stave to be outside the other part:

The space in which a rest centres, or its distance from the stave, should be on the same level as surrounding pitches. Thus the semibreve rests in the following example move lines to reflect the changing position of surrounding pitches. When a note is on a ledger line, place the rests above the top stave-space (or below the bottom stave-space for notes on ledger lines beneath the stave):

Rests that are part of a beat (marked ⊓) should align horizontally:

When the position of a rest is displaced by a note of the other part, the rest moves further away from the stave. This applies to all the rests in the following example:

When the notation becomes this complicated, it is better to separate the parts on to individual staves, for clarity.

Dotted rests

The dot remains in the same position relative to the rest, regardless of the rest's position on the stave:

Rests on a single line

The breve rest hangs from the line (as a semibreve rest does). The middle of the crotchet rest or its base hook intersects the line:

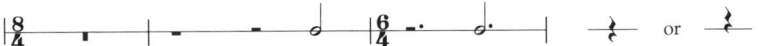

For quaver rests and shorter values, either the bottom stroke intersects the line, or the hooks are placed either side of the line:

(For use of rests, see *Grouping rests according to the metre*, p. 160.)

Barlines

Single barlines

The barline is thicker than a stave-line, and therefore conspicuously thicker than a stem. It is very important that barlines stand out from stems, especially when there are long, complicated bars in a single-stave instrumental part.

A barline connects all staves at the beginning of a system. This particular barline is called the systemic barline. A single-stave part does not have this barline at the beginning of the stave. (A single stave in a full score does, however.)

Thin double barlines

These mark divisions between sections in a piece. They are of ordinary barline thickness, and are placed about ¾ stave-space apart.

It is misleading to use them with every metre change, as they will appear to indicate new sections.

When two movements follow one another without a break, the end of the first movement takes a thin double barline (if at a system break, then together with advance warning of any change of clef, key and time signature for the new movement).

Final barlines

The thick final line is of beam thickness. The thin barline is placed ½ stave-space before it. The final double barline is used only at the end of a movement.

(See also *Da Capo and Dal Segno layouts: Double barlines*, p. 240.)

Repeat barlines

These use the final double barline design together with repeat dots. At a barline, the repeat sign replaces the barline (see *Placing repeat barlines*, p. 233.)

Rhythmic spacing

Musicians rely heavily on good spacing to read rhythm. Poor horizontal spacing is often the main problem of badly presented music and hinders the reading of it.

Durations should be spaced in relative proportion to each other, each value taking only a little more space than the next shortest value (units of relative measurement are given as a guide to the spacing proportions):

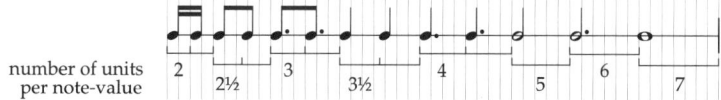

Note-values and rests are spaced in exact mathematical ratio only when metrical notation is superseded by literal time-space notation, in which a given horizontal length represents duration.

Because of the excessive space it would afford to longer durations, notes of unequal length are not spaced in mathematically exact proportion. Instead, longer durations are compressed to create more even spacing. Notes or rests of different durations should have just enough space to appear longer or shorter than those surrounding them, although in reality they may be virtually equidistant. Musicians are so used to this spacing that they appreciate the slightest differences:

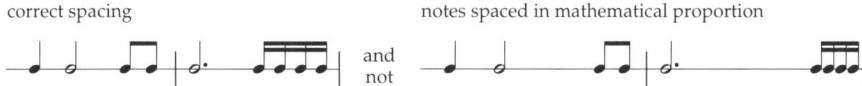

The eye will confuse rhythms only when the relative distance between notes or rests contradicts their duration. The following example demonstrates how poor spacing hinders reading the rhythm:

Each longer value of the above example should have more space than its shorter neighbour (a), or at least as much (b):

Notes of equal duration require equal spacing for an entire system, even when the speed of the note-values changes:

The uniform space allotted to a note-value can vary from system to system according to the number of bars on that system. For a passage of like rhythms, where the number of notational symbols is roughly equal, aim to place a similar number of bars on adjacent systems. Where the density of the notation increases, the uniform space for a note-value may need to be noticeably different from that of an adjacent system:

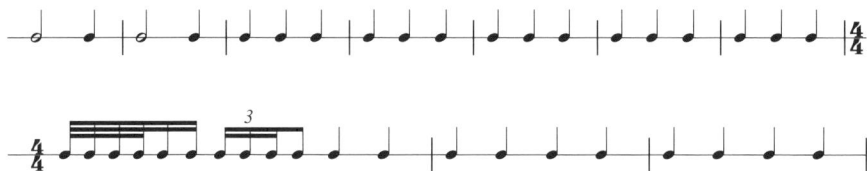

The barline may go where the position of the next beat would be. It usually goes slightly earlier, especially where space is limited.

In certain cases, spacing should be adjusted to create an illusion of evenness. Adjacent stems 'back to back' can otherwise look too close together (marked *). Notes with stems away from each other can look too far apart (marked ↑):

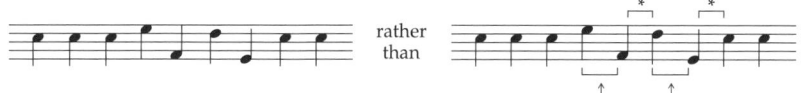

Notes of bar-length duration

In traditional engraving, when a bar contains a single note and there are no other durations in any part, the note is placed just left of the centre of the bar. Such bars, by definition, are usually fairly narrow. This spacing creates a better balance than a single note positioned at the beginning of the bar:

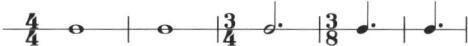

In widely spaced bars, the note can be placed closer to the barline so as not to appear isolated.

When there are other durations in other parts, the single duration is placed at the beginning of the bar as normal.

Spacing symbols

The essence of good layout is evenly spaced symbols, as this is what the eye most easily assimilates. Therefore, ideally, each system should contain a comparable number of symbols (notes or other notational characters). The spacing of symbols may widen or narrow according to how numerous they are on a system. Where space is limited, the distance between characters should not be less than ½ stave-space and no characters should collide.

The following spacing is recommended, as this illustrates traditional engraving practice.

Beginning of the system

Separate the clef, key signature, time signature by 1–1½ stave-spaces.

The greatest distance between symbols should precede the first note. For a note without an accidental, allow 2–3 stave-spaces:

Notes can be placed slightly closer to a time signature than to a clef or key signature. An accidental must be sufficiently far from a clef or a key signature for it not to be mistaken for one:

A first note or chord with an accidental may move closer to the preceding symbol(s). When further accidentals are added, these move closer to the clef. However, an accidental should never be closer to a preceding symbol than one stave-space:

Recommended distances before first note

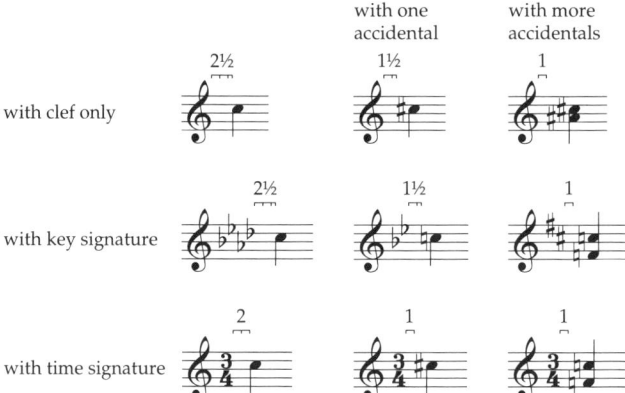

An accidental closes up as far as possible to its following note or fellow accidental without colliding (see also *Arranging accidentals for chords*, p. 87).

Mid-system

Allow a stave-space after a clef and on either side of a barline before a notational symbol. It is good practice to allow two spaces after a time signature or key signature. Where a barline comes before the end of the stave, allow a stave-space at the end of the stave:

Where space is limited, an accidental or grace note may be closed up to within ½ space of a barline. Stems must never come closer to a barline than one space, because the close parallel lines are difficult to read:

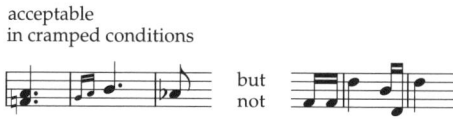

ADDITIONAL CLEFS AND ACCIDENTALS

Where notes are spaced close together, the addition of clef changes and accidentals can distort the rhythmic spacing. Although it is sometimes better to increase the spacing between notes to accommodate the clefs and accidentals, this wider spacing can be unhelpful, as well as impractical. Instead, reduce the space around clefs and accidentals to ½ space, to minimize distortion:

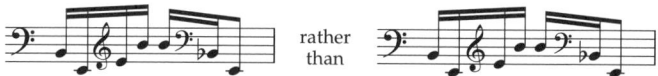

Where possible, note-spacing should remain unaffected by the addition of accidentals. One accidental can usually be accommodated (a) unless notes are very close together (b):

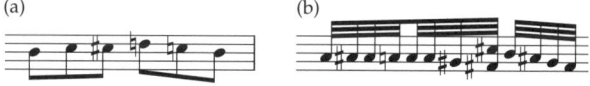

Two or more accidentals usually require extra space (a); it is better not to create wider spacing so as to space notes at identical intervals, as this disrupts the even spread of symbols (b):

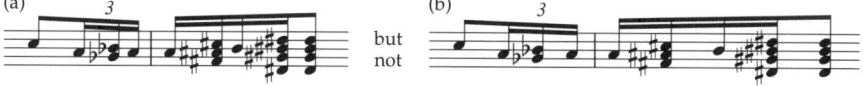

2

Chords – Dotted Notes – Ties

CONTENTS

CHORDS 47

Single-stemmed chords 47

Adjacent-note chords 48

Chords with single-stemmed unison notes 50

Double-stemmed writing 52

DOTTED NOTES 54

Chords 55

Double stems 56

Dotted unisons 58

TIES 60

Tie design 60

Tie direction for single notes 64

Tie direction for single-stemmed chords 65

Tie direction in double-stemmed writing 67

Tied unisons 69

Tie direction for single-stemmed moving chords 70

Open ties 72

Chords

Single-stemmed chords

Two or more notes of the same duration are combined onto one stem to form a chord:

Notes of different duration can be combined onto one stem for a chord only in string writing:

This is because the bow can sustain only two notes at once.

In all other cases, notes of different duration must take separate stems. The upper part takes up-stems, and the lower part takes down-stems (see *Double-stemmed writing*, p. 52):

Stem direction

The notehead furthest away from the centre of the stave determines the stem direction. When this note is above the middle line, the chord takes a down-stem; when the note is below the middle line, the chord takes an up-stem:

Stems joining noteheads that are equidistant from the centre of the stave can go in either direction, although many editions use only down-stems:

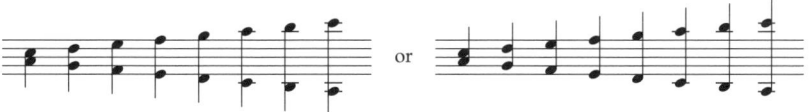

As with stem direction of single notes (see *Stem direction*, p. 13), the direction may be determined by context. The aim is to achieve a consistent stem direction within a phrase, bar or half-bar:

CHORDS WITH THREE OR MORE NOTES

The stem direction is still determined by whichever of the chord's outer notes is furthest from the centre of the stave:

Where the outer notes are equidistant from the centre of the stave, stem direction is determined by the position of the majority of notes. When the majority is above the middle stave-line, the chord takes a down stem; when the majority is below the middle line, the chord takes an up-stem:

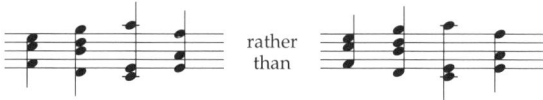

The following chords have all notes equidistant from the centre of the stave and so can take either stem direction:

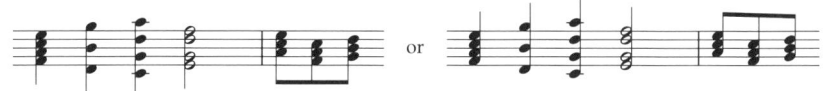

Adjacent-note chords

Single stems

TWO ADJACENT NOTES

To write intervals a second apart, place the lower note on the left-hand side of the stem, the upper note on the right-hand side:

Adjacent-note chords slope diagonally from bottom left to top right, even when this means a repeated note changes stem-side from chord to chord:

ADJACENT-NOTE CHORDS 49

MORE THAN TWO ADJACENT NOTES

The majority of notes fall on the 'correct' side of the stem. Thus when there are an odd number of notes, the lowest note goes on the left-hand side for up-stems, and on the right-hand side for down-stems:

When there is an even number of notes, the lowest note always goes on the left-hand side of the stem:

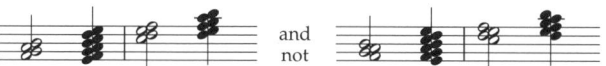

The French system of placing the highest and lowest notes on the 'correct' side of the stem should not be followed, since often this forces the lower of two adjacent notes to the right (rather than to the left) side of the stem:

Double stems

Arrange chords so that notes on the 'correct' side of each stem align vertically:

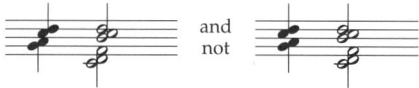

(This same principle should be used to align adjacent-note chords in a score.)

The only exception is when a tone or semitone separates the two parts. In this case, the lower part is displaced to the right (if the parts are vertically aligned, it is hard to tell which note belongs to which part):

(See also *Offsetting unison and adjacent noteheads*, p. 53.)

Stemless notes

Stemless noteheads are arranged as if they were stemmed:

Chords with single-stemmed unison notes

Perfect unisons

Place one notehead each side of the stem:

(For *Dotted unisons*, see p. 58.)

Altered unisons

Place each notehead after its own accidental in ascending chromatic order (flat to sharp).

Usually a note is displaced to the right of a chord, and joined to the vertical stem by a diagonal one. Position the diagonal so as to avoid cutting through (and thereby obscuring) the second accidental:

Extend the vertical stem beyond the point where the diagonal joins it. Any tails or beams should be clear of the diagonal stem:

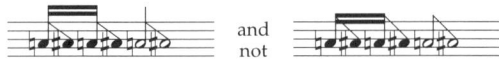

Occasionally, it is more convenient to displace a note before the rest of the chord, for example when there is more space available before rather than after the chord. Another part would align with the stem:

A two-note chord can, alternatively, splay out from the vertical stem in both directions, using a branching stem:

In very cramped conditions, it is acceptable to place one notehead each side of the stem with both accidentals before both notes. This notation is compact but much less clear, since an accidental is always best placed beside the notehead to which it applies. If this layout is used, both notes must have accidentals, or the two pitches will appear to be the same. The order of accidentals for a chord containing a sharp and a natural sign is ♯♮, since ♮♯ might appear to be a sharp cancelling a double-sharp sign:

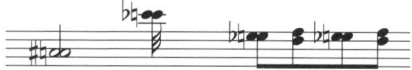

An accidental must never be placed after the note to which it refers, since a note cannot be modified once it has been sounded:

(See also *Accidentals in double-stemmed writing: Altered unisons*, p. 91.)

In a note cluster

All noteheads must be attached to a stem so that they are immediately identified as part of the chord. It is not enough that a notehead touches another notehead:

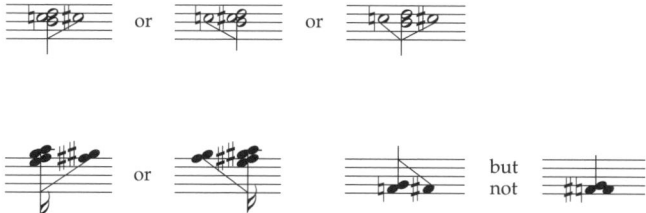

STEMLESS NOTES

A square bracket should encompass simultaneous notes. Align another part with the first notehead, or otherwise where the stem of an adjacent-note chord would be:

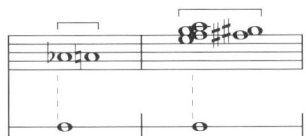

Double-stemmed writing

The upper part always takes up-stems, the lower part down-stems, even when pitches overlap (see *Overlapping parts*, p. 53).

Unisons

Two parts with the same note-value may share a notehead as long as they take two stems:

Notes without stems take a separate notehead for each part:

A black notehead can be shared by any black-note durations:

Semibreves, minims and black noteheads should be kept separate from each other:

(See also *Dotted unisons*, p. 58.)

Offsetting unison and adjacent noteheads

Offset the lower part to the right. Vertically align the upper part with a part on another stave:

Exceptions to this rule occur when parts overlap (see below; also, *Overlapping parts*, p. 57); and when double-stemmed adjacent or unison notes have only one dotted part (see *Adjacent notes*, p. 56, and *Dotted unisons: One part dotted*, p. 59).

Keep noteheads separate; stems should not touch. Semibreves in particular should not appear to be joined to stems:

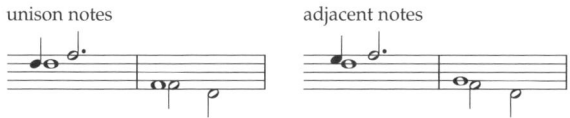

Some editions reverse the order of noteheads so that the semibreve is never adjacent to a stem. The part on the left aligns vertically with a part on another stave (this is the case whichever the notehead arrangement):

Overlapping parts

Place a down-stemmed part to the left so that noteheads can overlap. Slightly separate the parts so that the stems do not appear to include both notes. As with adjacent and unison noteheads, it is the part on the left that aligns with a part on another stave:

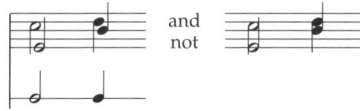

This is more compact than the following:

Place a down-stemmed part to the left for overlapping adjacent notes:

Overlapping semibreves must be divided into stemmed notes in order to show part progression:

(For arrangement with ledger-line notes, see *Double-stemmed adjacent notes and overlapping parts*, p. 27.)

Dotted Notes

Most traditional engraving uses a duration dot that is larger than a staccato dot – often twice the size.

Placing dots relative to noteheads

Place the dot close to its notehead so that it can be spotted immediately – usually a half stave-space's distance.

Double and triple dots should be placed close together and evenly spaced:

When notes are in a space, place the dot in the middle of that space. When notes are on a line, place the dot in the space above:

(See also *Double stems*, p. 56.)

Dotted notes on ledger lines follow the same principle. The dot moves above the ledger line when the note is on a line:

Up-stemmed notes with tails: should the end of a tail coincide with the position of the dot and thereby obscure it, it is acceptable to move the dot to the right of the tail:

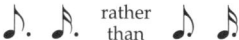

It is equally acceptable to lengthen the stem.

Chords

Every notehead in a chord must take a duration dot. Vertically align the dots after the chord:

Adjacent-note chords

When the upper note is on a line, the dot moves up into the next stave-space, as usual. When the lower note is on a line, the dot drops to the lower space:

Each dot should always have a stave-space to itself. This same spacing applies to chords on ledger lines as well, where dots should not be bunched up just because there are no stave lines to separate them into individual spaces (see following example).

A dot may need to move a stave-space away from its notehead. Do not align the dots horizontally, as this gives double-dotted value to the notes:

Centre the dots on the chord, rather than placing them in one direction, away from the chord:

When a dot is forced to be two or more stave-spaces from the chord, its function becomes less relevant. In such cases, use only as many dots as cover the number of stave-spaces taken up by the chord:

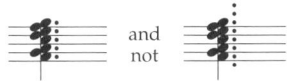

Double stems

LOWER PART ON A LINE

Drop the dot into the space below the lower part:

When the voices are close together, this avoids ambiguity as to which part the dot belongs:

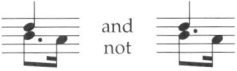

Adjacent notes

Both parts dotted: the upper dot is usually aligned with the lower dot after both parts (this layout is most compact), although it is acceptable to place each dot closer to each notehead:

One part dotted: each dot is placed next to its notehead, even though this may force a gap between the parts (see bar 1); a dot should not be separated from its notehead by the adjacent note:

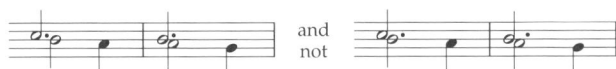

When the upper part is on a line, the upper dot may be placed above the lower notehead (see previous example, bar 2). However, so that the duration dot does not look like a staccato marking for the lower part, some editions place dotted upper notes to the right. Thus the dot is clear of both parts:

(See also *Overlapping adjacent notes*, below.)

CHORDS WITH ADJACENT NOTES

Align dots vertically for each part, independently of other chords:

Overlapping parts

Where only one part is dotted, do not separate a dot from its notehead by placing a stem in between:

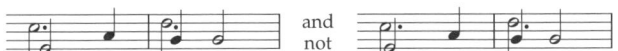

Where both parts are dotted and conditions are cramped, the layout is more compact if both dots follow both notes:

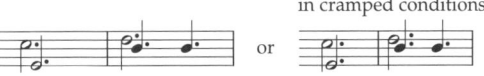

OVERLAPPING ADJACENT NOTES

Both parts dotted: the parts may overlap:

One part dotted: the parts should not overlap. Place a dotted up-stemmed part to the left and separate the parts with the dot. If the up-stemmed part goes to the right, it will look as if the down-stemmed part takes the dot:

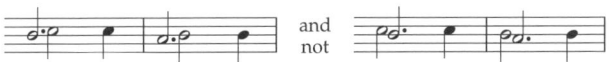

For a dotted down-stemmed part on a line, the dot is forced into the space above, to be clear of the up-stemmed part:

OVERLAPPING CHORDS

Place the dots beside each chord so that they are not separated from their noteheads by the other part, unless space is limited:

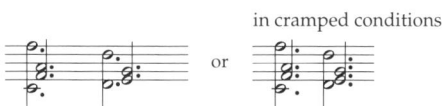

Dotted unisons

Single stems

Each notehead requires a dot. Each dot must have a separate stave-space, even though the noteheads are in the same space or on the same line; they will otherwise appear to be double-dotted:

CHORDS WITH A PRONGED STEM

It is best to place the dots after each notehead (they are most visible in this arrangement) except in cramped conditions:

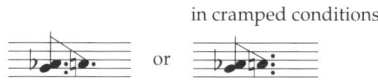

Double stems

BOTH PARTS DOTTED

A double-stemmed unison that has one notehead requires only one dot:

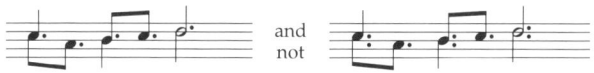

However, the unison semibreve requires two noteheads and therefore each notehead should take a dot:

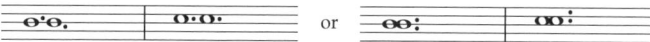

Unless conditions are cramped, notes of different duration take a dot beside each notehead:

ONE PART DOTTED

It is acceptable for the dotted note to share a notehead with a note without a dot as long as the rhythm of both parts is absolutely clear:

(This is a useful convention for repeated patterns in keyboard music.)

Should the rhythms appear ambiguous (the example above may well be considered inadequate), use separate noteheads as this will always be the clearest arrangement:

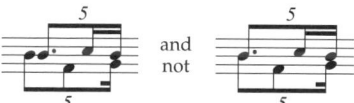

The normal arrangement is to place the upper part to the left:

However, there are two other equally valid approaches.

The first approach is to place the part without the dot first, to the left, so that the notes can close up. The reader infers that the dot applies to only the right-hand part, because otherwise the two parts would share the same notehead:

The other approach is to clarify that only one part is dotted by placing the dotted value first. Thus the dot separates the two noteheads:

On ledger lines: when the part placed first is dotted, separate the ledger lines. The ledger lines are not separated when only the second part takes a dot:

TIES

The function of a tie is to show the absence of rearticulation.

Tie design

The design of the tie, the curve and the gradation of the line, is a distinctive component of the appearance of the music.

A tie is a tapered arc, symmetrical in shape, which extends between two noteheads of identical pitch. Two enharmonically equivalent pitches may also be joined by a tie:

Square brackets should not be used as ties.

The tie and slur (phrase mark) have the same design, although ties tend to have a flatter arc, to allow room for slurs and to differentiate the two.

The tie extends from notehead to notehead: if one or both ends point to a stem, the arc becomes a slur:

The tie should almost touch each notehead. An arc further away from the noteheads may be taken for a slur:

(See *Slurs*, p. 109.)

Curve of the tie

The curve of the tie should be sufficiently round to be conspicuous through a stave-line. Ideally, a shallow tie is 1–1½ stave-spaces deep.

The centre of the curve should not coincide with a stave-line, since the tie then becomes less conspicuous. This means that ties drawn within the stave will usually cut through a stave-line:

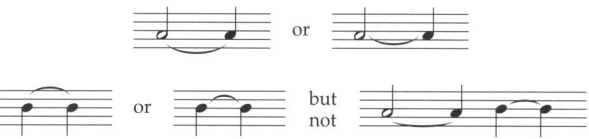

Ties are generally confined within one stave-space when they are very short, and when they must be flattened to avoid another part:

Should it be impossible to add a tie without obscuring a notehead, a tie may be divided (see example *Dividing ties*, p. 133).

The curve of a long tie is flattened to prevent excessively variable curve heights between ties:

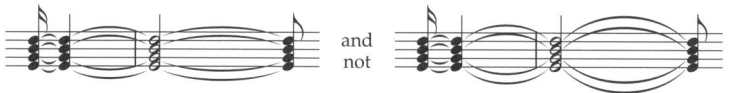

Note that when chords have stems with tails (as above), it is best to lengthen the stem to avoid tails and ties colliding.

Positioning ends of tie relative to notehead

The exact position of the ends of a tie may vary according to surrounding notation.

Where there is plenty of space and no articulation to implement, the tie starts and finishes at the centre of the notehead:

Where the tie needs to be brought closer to the notehead (e.g. to allow space for articulation), the ends of the tie align with the edge of the notehead:

(See also *Placing articulation and slurs with ties*, below.)

The tie may start slightly after and finish slightly before the notehead. When notes are in spaces, this enables the ends of a tie to be brought into the same space as the notehead:

Such positioning is often necessary for tied chords (see *Placing ties on chords*, opposite). Make ties between tightly spaced notes as long as possible, in order to have them most conspicuous:

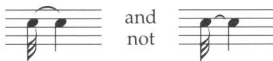

PLACING ARTICULATION AND SLURS WITH TIES

So that a tie does not collide with articulation or slurs, the ends of the tie align with the edge of the notehead (a) or else start slightly after and finish slightly before the notehead (b):

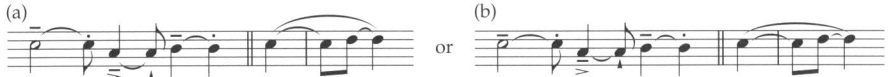

TIE DESIGN

A TIE INTERSECTING A STEM

A tie intersects a stem only under exceptional circumstances, e.g. when two parts overlap (see *Overlapping parts*, p. 67). In all other circumstances the tie should fall short of the following stem:

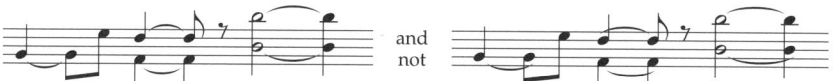

Placing ties on chords

MULTIPLE-NOTE CHORDS

Inner ties must start after and finish before each notehead. Outer ties may be drawn parallel to this, so that all ties are the same length (a). It is equally acceptable for the outer ties to be full length (b):

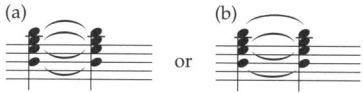

For close-position chords, it is best if ties start in the same stave-space as the notehead, so that they are clearly seen to be attached to the correct note:

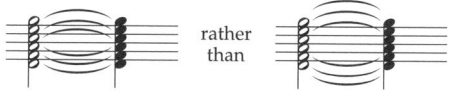

ADJACENT-NOTE CHORDS

It is usually clearer to start each tie close to each notehead, rather than to align all ties after all notes:

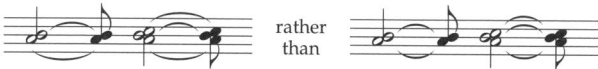

(See also *Tied unisons*, p. 69.)

Placing ties with dotted notes

SINGLE NOTES

Place the dot within the tie – the tie does not follow the dot. Curve the tie sufficiently to avoid obscuring the dot:

CHORDS

Position ties so that no dot is obscured.

Ties may start immediately after each notehead, in between the duration dots, as long as they will fit without colliding: (a) and not (d). Otherwise inner ties should start after the dots (b). Ties for outer notes may follow the position of inner ties if preferred, but this may place these ties rather far from their noteheads (c):

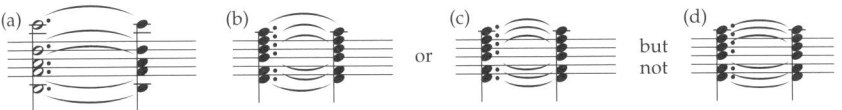

Tie direction for single notes

Stems in one direction

A tie curves away from the stems of the notes:

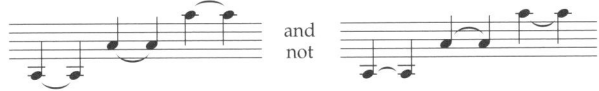

A tie between stemless notes behaves as if stems were present:

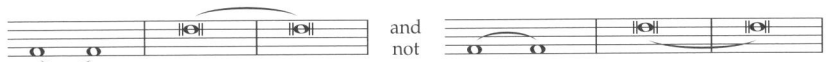

Consecutive stems in opposite directions

Ties curve away from the middle stave-line:

To curve all ties upwards for notes below the middle line, as some editions do, creates a collision between a tie and the tail of an up-stemmed first note:

(However, this may be unavoidable in double-stemmed writing – see p. 67.)

Ties over a system break

A tie stops short of the last barline of a system. At the start of a new system the tie begins after the clef, key signature and time signature.

Tie direction remains consistent over the system break and should not be altered when the notes on either side of it take opposite stem direction:

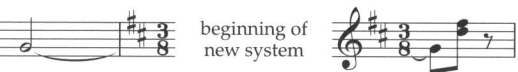

Over a system break, the open-ended tie keeps its symmetrical shape. This symmetrical curve ensures it is not mistaken for a slur nor a glissando line:

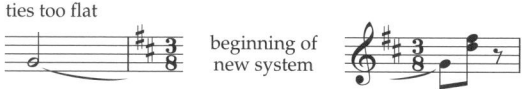

(See example *Slurs and ties over a system break*, p. 112.)

Tie direction for single-stemmed chords

Two notes on a stem: the ties curve in opposite directions:

An even number of ties: equal numbers of ties curve in each direction:

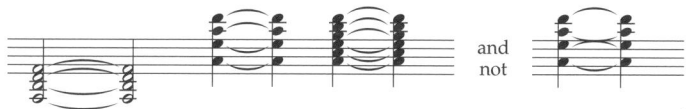

An odd number of ties: the majority of ties curve away from the stem:

Some editions tie middle notes of both odd- and even-note chords according to their position on the stave. Ties for notes on and above the middle stave-line curve upwards, ties for notes below the middle line curve downwards:

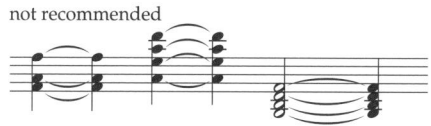

(See also *Adjacent notes*, p. 66.)

DISTANCE APART OF TIES

Place ties that are in the same direction a minimum of one stave-space apart. This applies to ties both on and outside the stave. One tie per stave-space prevents the ties from obscuring stave-lines or merging together:

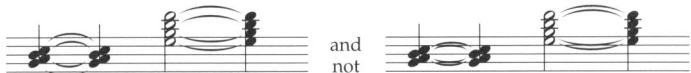

ON LEDGER LINES

Either flatten the ties (a) or move them horizontally further from the note-heads (b) in order to avoid them touching ledger lines (c):

Adjacent notes

Adjacent-note ties are curved away from each other. This avoids two ties close together curving in the same direction. The adjacent notes dictate the direction of all other ties in the chord, overruling the usual tie-direction conventions for the rest of the chord:

Pairs of adjacent notes: each pair may take opposite tie directions as long as the middle ties do not collide nor overlap:

Consecutive adjacent notes: curve parallel ties in both directions away from the middle of the chord. Position the ties outwards from the centre of the chord, one per stave-space. Each tied note must have a tie; therefore the ties at the edges of the chord will be progressively further away vertically from the notes to which they refer:

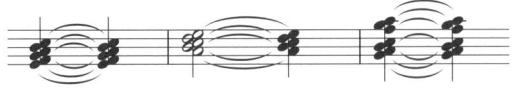

Tie direction in double-stemmed writing

The upper part takes upward-curving ties, the lower part downward-curving ties:

This applies to all the notes on one stem:

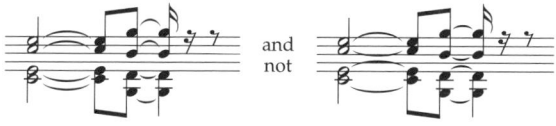

Overlapping parts

One part tied: when the parts are not tied simultaneously, the ties curve towards their stems as normal:

Where possible, place the parts so that a stem does not come between a note and its tie. This may involve reversing the usual arrangement of parts (marked *):

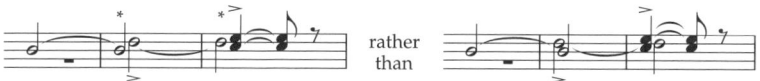

Both parts tied: ties may curve away from their stems if necessary, so that they are clear of each other:

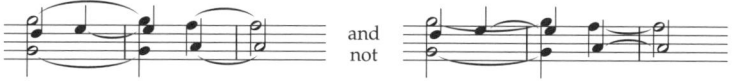

One tie should never intersect another, since this is visually confusing: either reverse normal tie direction (as above) or else divide up the tie (see first example under *With ledger lines*, p. 68).

Note that the tie may cut through the stem of the other part (as in the previous example), rather than curve a long way from the notehead, which makes the tie look too similar to a slur:

A stem should not end at the point it meets the tie. Either shorten or lengthen the stem. A tie may cut through the stems of a beamed group as long as the tie is sufficiently curved and does not look like another beam (bars 1–2):

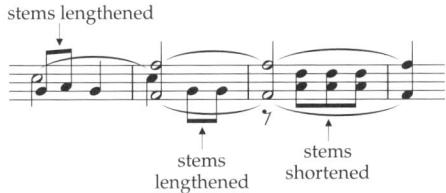

WITH LEDGER LINES

A tie should not pass between ledger lines. A tie by nature should be kept as flat as possible, to distinguish it from a slur. Therefore it is sometimes clearest to break the tie:

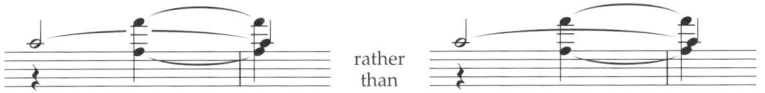

When a tie is not required to overlap with another, it is clearest not to break it. It may be moved further from the notes while being kept reasonably flat (a). When the curve of the tie is too rounded, it looks too much like a slur (b):

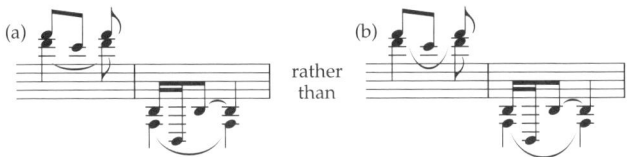

Whether or not the parts overlap, never allow a tie to intersect the other part's ledger lines.

Tied unisons

Single stems

PERFECT UNISONS

Each notehead requires its own tie.

The ties should point to and from each notehead, with the upper tie for the note on the left and the lower tie for the note on the right:

A stem should not intersect a tie:

Ties must not overlap nor cross; it is better to point the ties to the 'wrong' notehead:

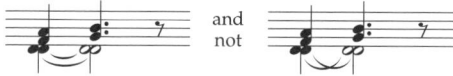

and
not

ALTERED UNISONS

Each tie should be drawn between its own noteheads:

Double stems

Each part must have its own tie, even though there is only one notehead and one duration dot:

A single tie indicates that only one part is tied; however, when this is the case, it is clearest to use two noteheads:

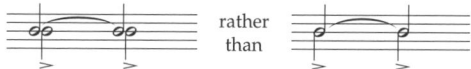

rather
than

When the parts have different durations, it is acceptable to reverse the order of noteheads so that a notehead can be nearer its tie:

When one part is also dotted, the part with the dot may go to the right, so that the notes can close up:

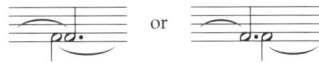

Tie direction for single-stemmed moving chords

For clarity, a moving part usually takes a separate stem, but where this is not possible, tied and untied notes may appear on the same stem. To draw attention to a note-change in a chord, curve ties away from an added or released note:

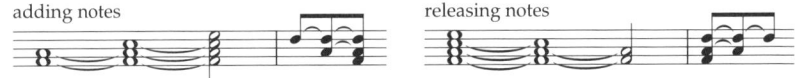

When one note is added whilst another is released on alternate sides of a tied note, obviously the tie direction cannot be curved away from both. Usually the tie is curved away from a note added for the second chord:

The tie can be curved towards the added note if it would otherwise be unclear which note was tied:

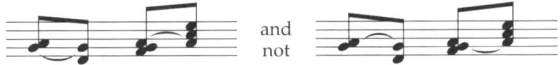

A passage of such chords looks clearest when all ties are placed in one direction:

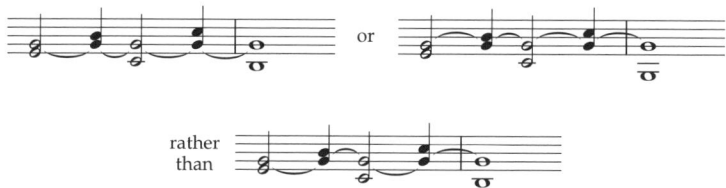

Ties are placed conventionally when notes are added or released simultaneously above and below the tied note:

Curve a tie away from an added note with an accidental, so that the two do not collide:

WITH SLURS

When a slur connects chords, place ties and slurs in opposite directions so as to be clearly distinguishable from one another:

CHORDS TIED WITHOUT A CHANGE OF PITCH

The ties for unchanging chords revert to their conventional positions (marked ↓):

(See also *Arpeggiated chords notated as consecutive pitches,* p. 133; for use of ties with tremolos, see *Ties,* p. 225.)

Open ties

A short, open (or 'incomplete') tie is used to show that a note is sustained beyond its written duration. This is also indicated *laissez vibrer* (see below).

A long tie extending to a rest or barline indicates that a note should be held for its full length:

A short open-ended tie extending from the notehead is used in some French editions to replace the longer complete tie. This should not be used, as it does not show the progression of the tied note sufficiently clearly:

Such ties should be used only where no other solution is practical.

Laissez vibrer

(French, 'leave to vibrate', Italian: *lasciar vibrare*; abbrev. *l.v.*)

This is an instruction not to damp an instrument that has natural sustaining resonance. The instruction applies to sounds that are sustained naturally by an instrument, not held manually, and which are not to be damped until indicated (if at all).

The instruction *l.v. sempre* specifies that no notes in a passage are to be damped.

The initial note is best written as a single note-value, as this is easiest to read; *l.v.* is written after the note. This may be accompanied by an open tie, although *l.v.* or a tie alone is sufficient:

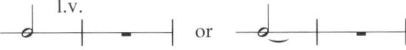

The instruction *l.v. al niente* indicates that the sound should be allowed to die away to nothing.

When a sound is to be damped later on, the continuing resonance is indicated with open ties over or after subsequent barlines (but see also *Notes sustained with a pedal*, opposite). Add rests to make up the value of incomplete bars (see bar 4). Rests may be omitted for whole bars, but are best added for completeness:

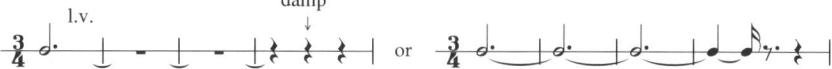

Rests may be divided up to show a damping or pedal release point in the middle of a bar (as above).

It is better not to indicate the termination (release) point with a tied note-value, unless all durations are written in full, since at a quick glance it may look as if the sound should be re-articulated:

NOTES SUSTAINED WITH A PEDAL

Instruments that can sustain notes with pedals (piano, celesta, vibraphone) do not require *l.v.* ties for notes that are sustained in this way, since pedal markings must be indicated in any case. Once a note is struck, the sound will be sustained until the pedal is released. Continued notation of the sustained notes for the duration of the pedal is unnecessarily complicated:

3
Accidentals and Key Signatures

CONTENTS

ACCIDENTALS 77

Design 77

Placing 78

Using accidentals 78

Using accidentals in an atonal context 85

Arranging accidentals for chords 87

Accidentals in double-stemmed writing 90

KEY SIGNATURES 91

Placing and order of accidentals 91

Spacing 92

Key changes 92

Key signatures in non-tonal or polytonal music 93

MICROTONES 94

Quarter-tones 94

Other microtones 96

Cancelling microtonal alteration 98

Accidentals

The first section below describes the standard accidental symbols in detail so as to show their required proportion to the stave and their placing on it. This is critical: the slightest vertical displacement of an accidental will cause confusion, as note and accidental will appear to refer to different pitches. Accidentals that are too small are difficult to read as they start to look alike from a distance or in bad light.

Design

The sharp: the crossbars are slightly thinner than the depth of a beam. They are parallel, each slightly angled, so that when the sharp is placed in a stave-space, the top left of each crossbar hangs from the line, the bottom right sits on the line. The width of the sharp symbol is one stave-space or a little more. The vertical strokes are about half a stave-space apart. They extend just less than one stave-space each side of the crossbar. The right stroke is set higher than the left, to follow the angle of the crossbars:

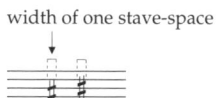

The flat: the vertical stem is about 2½ stave-spaces long. The width of the bowl is slightly less than one stave-space and in depth should fill a stave-space when positioned in one:

The natural: the crossbars are the same thickness as those of the sharp. When a natural sits in a stave-space, the crossbars intersect the stave-lines in the same way as the crossbars of a sharp. The natural is slightly less than one stave-space wide. Its vertical strokes extend one stave-space beyond the crossbars:

The double flat: the two flat signs are placed together and (usually) touching:

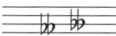

The double sharp: this is a stylized cross, a stave-space in width and height:

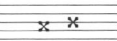

An accidental is scaled down in size only when placed before a grace note (see *Design*, p. 125), or a cue note.

Placing

ON THE STAVE

The central portion of an accidental symbol must precisely fill a stave-space, or be centred on a line. Take great care when assigning accidentals to notes on ledger lines – without the guidance of the stave it is easy to place an accidental ambiguously:

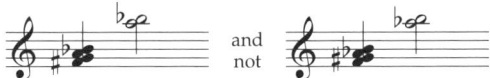

PROXIMITY TO NOTES

An accidental should be as close as possible to the note it precedes. Allow sufficient space to ensure that an accidental does not collide with a symbol that precedes it, or it will become illegible:

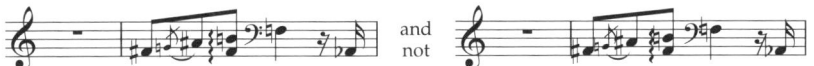

(See *Spacing symbols*, p. 41.)

Using accidentals

Changes of clef, octave and stave

An accidental holds good for the duration of a bar. It applies only to the pitch at which it is written: each additional octave requires a further accidental.

CLEF CHANGES

An accidental holds good only in the clef in which it is written. A change of clef requires a further accidental for a note of the same pitch (see the following example, bar 1, third beat, left hand).

OCTAVE CHANGES

Repeat an accidental if sounding at a different octave, even when the same pitch is used with an octave sign – the location of the changed octave is likely to be different (see example below, bar 2, at ↓).

TWO OR MORE STAVES FOR ONE PLAYER

An accidental holds good only for the stave in which it is written. It should be confirmed (see ∗) or cancelled (✱) when it occurs in another stave in the same bar. When a note with an accidental is taken with the other hand in the same stave, the accidental holds good (bar 2, left hand) and does not need to be repeated.

Accidentals relevant to more than one part on a stave

The following conventions apply irrespectively of whether individual parts are stemmed separately or together.

SINGLE-INSTRUMENT PART

An accidental applies to all parts on a stave – it is not repeated for each separate part in a given bar. Similarly, a cancelled accidental applies to the same pitch in any of the parts:

PART FOR TWO OR MORE PERFORMERS

Choral music and orchestral parts often double up two (or more) parts on one stave in a score. For clarity, confirm or cancel each accidental in every part. This guarantees that essential accidentals are not omitted when instrumental parts are extracted, or when different voices read from a single stave in a vocal score.

Place an accidental for each affected part in turn, even if the same pitch appears consecutively in different parts:

3 Trumpets

An accidental that holds good in one part must be restated later in the bar if it has, in the meantime, been altered by another part:

2 Trumpets

Accidentals tied over a barline

An accidental holds good over a barline only for the duration of a tied note. A repeated pitch in the following bar must have an accidental:

OVER A SYSTEM BREAK

It is helpful to repeat an accidental on a tied note at the beginning of a new system so that the reader does not have to look back to a previous system to confirm the pitch. The tied accidental may be enclosed in brackets, although brackets may decrease the legibility of the accidental. For music with many tied chords, it is often better not to repeat accidentals, as they congest the beginning of the system.

If the accidental for the tied note is without brackets, a repeat of the pitch later in the bar does not require confirmation. This notation is preferable to repeating an accidental twice in a bar in close succession:

REPEATING TIED ACCIDENTALS AFTER EVERY BARLINE

This practice has been used to facilitate vertical reading in a score. However, it burdens the score with many extra accidentals and is not recommended.

Such practice should never be transferred to a part to be played or sung from, since the eye is triggered for action by the presentation of a new accidental.

A tied note looks as if it should be re-articulated and the tie appears to be a slur:

Cancelling accidentals

DOUBLE FLATS AND DOUBLE SHARPS

When a double flat is cancelled by a single flat, and a double sharp by a single sharp, the traditional practice of placing a natural sign before these is redundant, since a single flat or sharp sign cannot mean anything else:

AFTER THE BARLINE

The barline cancels an altered pitch. However, it is essential either to restate or cancel the accidental when the repeated pitch recurs immediately after the barline:

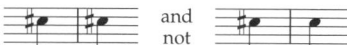

Otherwise the note after the barline should theoretically be a natural, but, in the absence of a natural sign, the reader will question whether the second bar has a missing sharp sign.

This practice holds good even when a key signature corrects the accidental:

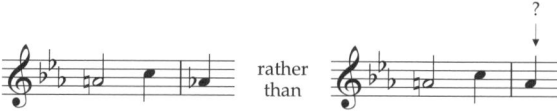

It is good practice to cancel an accidental in any part of the following bar:

except where there is an enharmonic change that makes such accidentals redundant:

In performance material, further accidentals may be added to a pitch that recurs within a few bars, to help avoid mistakes in reading:

(See also *Cautionary accidentals*, below.)

OCTAVE DISPLACEMENT

A pitch that occurs at a different octave should be confirmed or altered with an accidental:

When returning to a pitch after alteration at a different octave, confirm the original pitch with an accidental, to avoid ambiguity:

Cautionary accidentals

An accidental that is repeated later in a bar, even though it is not strictly necessary, is called a 'cautionary' (or 'reminder' or 'courtesy') accidental. Cautionary accidentals confirm the pitch of a note that might otherwise be questioned (see next paragraph). Atonal and highly chromatic idioms should include cautionary accidentals to assist accurate reading.

USES

Cautionary accidentals confirm whether an accidental earlier in the bar still holds good or not. In rehearsal or performance, the musician may not have time to look back through a long, highly chromatic bar to confirm whether a pitch has been altered by intervening accidentals.

Cautionary accidentals should confirm that diminished and augmented intervals are intentional:

They may also confirm that a dissonance with a player seated close by is correct. (An orchestral player will not normally have access to a full score to check this.) In vocal music, the singer should be alerted to all close dissonances (e.g. semitone intervals) between voices or with the accompaniment.

PLACING CAUTIONARY ACCIDENTALS

According to traditional practice, such accidentals are placed in brackets, to confirm that they are not strictly essential. This approach also clarifies that there is not a previously missing accidental in the bar:

However, since many bracketed accidentals (as in the example above) reduce overall legibility, the use of brackets is feasible only when there are just a few cautionary accidentals.

On a chord, each accidental takes a separate pair of brackets.

Brackets force extra horizontal space between the accidental and the surrounding notes, which interrupts consistent note-spacing. It is therefore better either to write all accidentals without brackets:

or, where horizontal space is limited, to place cautionary (but not essential) accidentals directly above their notes:

Square brackets around accidentals should be used only to indicate editorial additions in practical or scholarly editions. Editorial additions may, alternatively, be given as small-sized accidentals above their notes (in the manner illustrated above).

When highly chromatic music requires many cautionary accidentals to be used, it is always helpful to explain the accidental practice in the preface: e.g. 'accidentals apply through the bar, but are repeated for ease of reading'. Otherwise performers may query whether an accidental applies only to the note it precedes (see *Accidental systems*, p. 86).

Accidentals affecting grace notes

Accidentals hold good equally for grace notes and for measured notes. However, unless the measured note follows the grace note almost immediately (bar 2), for safety it is best to repeat an accidental for a measured note:

An accidental for a measured note is always deemed to hold good for a subsequent grace note:

A grace-note accidental is cancelled for a subsequent measured note (bar 1), and a full-sized accidental is cancelled for a subsequent grace note (bar 2):

Accidentals affecting ornaments

An altered pitch should be confirmed or cancelled for an ornament later in the bar. Place an accidental for an upper note above the ornament, below for a lower note:

E♭ confirmed   E♭ cancelled by ♮

An accidental indicated for an ornament should be confirmed or cancelled when the pitch is reiterated later in the bar as a measured note:

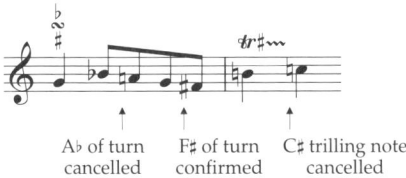

A♭ of turn   F♯ of turn   C♯ trilling note
cancelled   confirmed   cancelled

A key signature modifies the pitch of an ornament. To overrule a key signature an ornament requires an accidental:

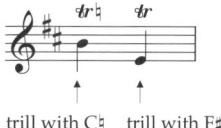

trill with C♮   trill with F♯

(See also *Trilling note*, p. 138.)

Using accidentals in an atonal context

Note-spelling

Notes are easiest to read and to pitch when they are spelled according to the following conventions, whether or not the music has a tonal context.

- Use the most familiar intervals – perfect, minor and major – rather than augmented and diminished intervals
- Chromatic-scale figures use sharps to ascend, flats to descend
- Spell stepwise figures as a scale, i.e. as adjacent pitch letters:

There is no reason to leave out double sharps and double flats if they clarify the harmonic sense:

Avoid enharmonic-spelling changes in the middle of a phrase where possible, since the awkward intervals this creates (marked ⌞⌟) are more difficult to read quickly:

In vocal music in particular, it is extremely important to spell notes with the most familiar melodic intervals. This enables the singer to 'hear' these intervals in advance of singing them.

Accidental systems

The traditional system of accidental use (as described in *Using accidentals*, p. 78) has been considered inadequate in certain contexts and replaced accordingly.

In densely chromatic idioms, unbarred and unmetred music, a reader might well expect an unconventional accidental system to be implemented. To avoid ambiguity in such cases it is a good idea to state in a preface when using traditional practice, e.g. 'accidentals hold good throughout the bar'.

AN ACCIDENTAL TO EVERY PITCH

This system was first adopted by composers of the Second Viennese School, for the specific intellectual reason that a note with an accidental was not simply an inflected version of a natural note but a pitch of equal status. The system also means that there is no opportunity to misread a pitch. In densely chromatic music – especially keyboard music – the system can be very helpful so as to keep track of accidentals within a bar.

When the system first came about, performers would have needed more assistance with the unfamiliar atonal medium. However, music so dense with accidentals looks forbiddingly difficult, and therefore reduces overall legibility (see Kurtág: *Kafka Fragments*). Furthermore, there is no longer the necessity to make the original intellectual point.

AN ACCIDENTAL APPLIES ONLY TO THE NOTE IT PRECEDES

Adopt this system only when there is sufficient time for performers to learn the music in advance – it is not recommended when there is minimal rehearsal time.

This system uses only sharp and flat signs, if strictly implemented, since a note without an accidental is a 'natural' pitch. Thus music with few black notes is much less cluttered by accidentals. It is advisable, however, to add a natural sign (if applicable) for an altered immediately repeated note, for safety:

The system can be modified, so that an accidental applies only to the note it precedes except in the case of an immediately repeated note or pattern of pitches, and notes joined by a beam. The extent of a 'repeated pattern of pitches' must always be clear: if in doubt, repeat accidentals. In the following example, it is unclear whether the last beat is a repeated pattern or whether the notes should be 'natural' pitches:

It is absolutely essential that an unconventional system is used consistently. Inconsistently cancelling accidentals causes ambiguity. To state 'accidentals apply to the note alone' for the following notation is misleading:

The natural to the E throws the pitch of the second D and B into question.

MUSIC WITHOUT BARLINES AND *AD LIBITUM* PASSAGES

In music without barlines, free passages and long cadenza bars there is no opportunity for barlines to cancel accidentals. Instead, use an accidental to apply to the note it precedes, to an immediately repeated note and within a beamed group. An accidental is repeated for subsequent notes, but cancelled only on immediately or closely following repeated notes. Add more accidentals to confirm pitches if necessary.

Arranging accidentals for chords

There is no hierarchical necessity to arrange accidentals in groups of sharps, naturals and flats. Rather, their order is determined by their position on the stave.

Place all accidentals as close as possible to the notes they precede, evenly spaced, but not too far apart:

All accidentals must be to the right of a barline. If they are bunched up and colliding with each other or with a barline, they will not be legible:

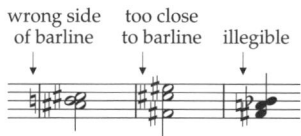

Two-note chords

The following rules are designed to give as compact an arrangement of accidentals as possible.

Pairs of accidentals an octave or more apart vertically align. Depending upon the exact length of the accidental symbol, accidentals a seventh and sixth apart can align as long as they do not collide or join up.

ACCIDENTALS A SEVENTH APART

Most combinations of accidentals a seventh apart can align without touching:

Otherwise slightly offset the lower accidental to the left:

ACCIDENTALS A SIXTH APART

When the upper note is a flat, accidentals can usually align. Otherwise the lower accidental is offset:

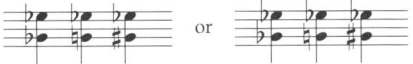

When the upper note is a sharp or natural, slightly offset the lower accidental so that the vertical strokes do not join up. The closest that two sharps may be placed together is so that the edges of their crossbars align vertically. The sharps cannot overlap, as the vertical strokes would join up:

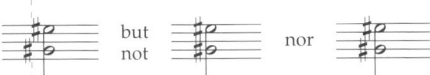

ACCIDENTALS A FIFTH OR LESS APART

The higher accidental goes closest to the chord, the lower one is offset to the left. Flat and natural signs a fourth or fifth apart may overlap as long as they do not join up:

Chords of three or more notes

CLOSE-POSITION CHORDS

Alternate the highest and lowest accidentals so as to allow a group of accidentals to be as compact as possible.

Place the highest accidental closest to the chord, followed by the lowest, moving left from the chord and alternating the highest and lowest of the remainder:

To place accidentals in descending order away from the chord (as seen in some editions) takes up more room, as each accidental needs fractionally more space to be clear of its neighbour:

CHORDS SPANNING A SEVENTH OR MORE

Align the accidentals for the outer notes closest to the chord. Offset further accidentals to the left, starting with the remaining highest, and alternating the highest and lowest, as in *Close-position chords*, above:

(See also *Chords with adjacent notes*, p. 90.)

WIDELY SPACED CHORDS OF FOUR OR MORE NOTES

When there are two overlapping sevenths, or wider intervals, align pairs of accidentals, as this takes up the least space:

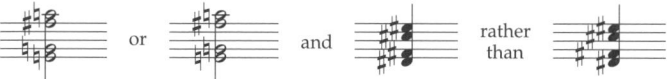

OCTAVE ACCIDENTALS

These are easiest to read when they align. Other accidentals may be offset to the left to allow for this:

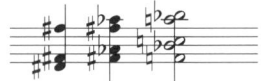

Chords with adjacent notes

It is visually helpful to place accidentals for adjacent notes in descending order, right to left, away from the chord, to reflect the arrangement of notes. This is especially helpful for pairs of adjacent notes (b). It is also acceptable to follow the conventional order of accidentals ((c) and (d)), as described above:

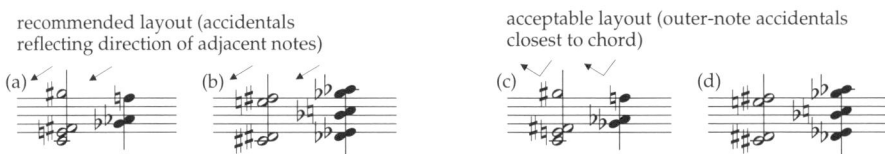

When there are several accidentals for a close-position chord, it is better to use the conventional arrangement, as the descending order of accidentals requires more space:

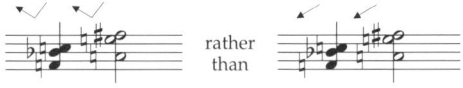

DOWN-STEMS

Move an accidental closer to the stem than a displaced note wherever there is room. This includes octave accidentals:

Accidentals in double-stemmed writing

Place accidentals before both parts, except for altered unisons (see opposite; see also *Altered unisons*, p. 50, and *In a note cluster*, p. 51).

The order of accidentals is the same as for single-stemmed chords, starting with the uppermost accidental closest to the notes:

ADJACENT NOTES AND OVERLAPPING PARTS

When the higher-pitched note is to the left of the two parts, the order of accidentals may be reversed to reflect the arrangement of notes. Thus each accidental is as close as possible to its note:

ALTERED UNISONS

Place each accidental beside each part so that it is clear which accidental belongs to which part:

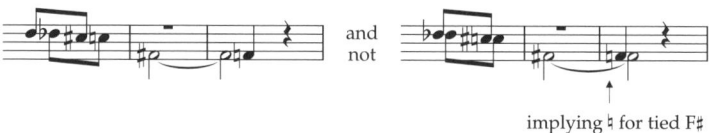

(If the upper note in bar 3 above joined to a unison note with the lower part, it would require a sharp sign placed before both notes.)

Key Signatures

Placing and order of accidentals

A key signature is placed at the beginning of the stave, after the clef and before a time signature. It should appear on every stave to which it is relevant, for as long as it is relevant.

The order of accidentals follows the 'cycle of fifths'. The arrangement is identical in each clef except for the tenor-clef layout of sharps:

Spacing

Sharps: the edges of the crossbars align vertically but do not overlap:

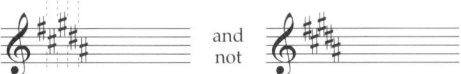

Flats: place each sign just far enough to the right for it not to touch the preceding flat. Flats in ascending fourths will fit in very close to each other – but keep the key signature evenly spaced, the stem of a second flat aligning with the right-hand edge of the previous flat. Do not overlap the flats, as the spacing will appear uneven:

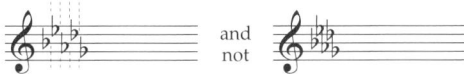

Key changes

Change a key signature after a barline. A double barline precedes the new key signature only if the key change coincides with a new musical section.

TRADITIONAL PRACTICE

Natural signs cancel a key signature before a new one is stated. The naturals should appear in the order of the key signature they are cancelling. Both the naturals and the new key signature go after the barline (old Russian editions place the naturals before the barline):

When a sharp or flat key leads to a key with fewer sharps or flats, the accidentals of the previous key signature are cancelled before the new key signature. However, some older editions (including nineteenth-century French editions) place the naturals after the new signature, to preserve the 'cycle of fifths' arrangement:

When a key change coincides with a system break, the cancelling naturals and the new key signature go at the end of the first system. The new system takes only the new key signature (see following example).

CONTEMPORARY PRACTICE

At a key change use only the new key signature. This gives a simpler result. A previous key signature requires cancelling with naturals only when the new section has no key signature:

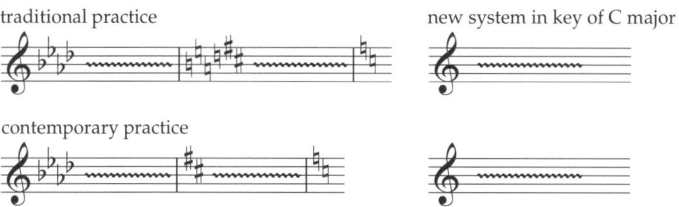

Simultaneous key and clef change

Place the new clef before the barline, the new key signature after the barline (and in the new clef):

Key signatures in non-tonal or polytonal music

Key signatures may be used to minimize repeated accidentals in any passage or movement that consistently uses the same accidental pitches.

CONVENTIONAL KEY SIGNATURES

In an ensemble work, an instrument may take its own key signature. (Stravinsky makes use of key signatures for individual instruments or selected sections of the orchestra in works such as *L'Oiseau de Feu*, *Chant du Rossignol*, and *Jeu de Cartes*. Holst also does so in *The Planets*.)

Harp music is written enharmonically according to its pedal settings and may use a completely different or enharmonically equivalent key to the rest of the ensemble. (A classic example is the C♭ major key signature used for both harps in the final movement of Bartók's *Concerto for Orchestra*, bars 256–265.)

An instrument on two (or more) staves can take an individual key signature for each stave. (Bartók employs this frequently, e.g. in 14 Bagatelles, op. 6; see also Cowell: *The Tides of Manaunaun*.)

UNCONVENTIONAL KEY SIGNATURES

Any sharp or flat may be selected as a key signature to alter all octaves of the selected pitches:

(Bartók uses many unconventional key signatures in the *Mikrokosmos* piano pieces.)

Microtones

No pitches other than the twelve chromatic degrees of the octave have standard notation. Symbols for any other pitches require a written definition. Arrows are a very convenient and logical symbol to show the raising and lowering of pitch.

Quarter-tones

Either arrows or fixed symbols (see p. 96) are used to define quarter-tones (hereafter ¼-tones).

Using arrows

An arrow can be attached to any accidental, or precede a note or accidental, pointing in the direction of the pitch modification. This is visually the most helpful symbol since it requires no memorizing.

The recommended symbol is an arrow attached to an accidental. Ensure that the arrowhead is sufficiently large to be visible on the stave. It is most convenient to attach the arrowhead to the sharp-sign verticals that project furthest from the centre of the symbol:

An arrow alone without an accidental may represent a pitch alteration (see first example below). However, when a conventional accidental precedes the microtone for the same pitch in the bar, an accidental must confirm or cancel the altered microtonal pitch:

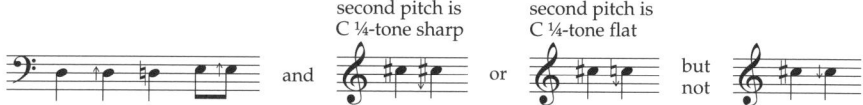

Arrows defining all quarter-tones

↑ = sharpen by a ¼-tone
↓ = flatten by a ¼-tone

Arrows can be attached to any accidental. This has the advantage of making all enharmonic equivalents available.

The following example shows enharmonic equivalents for each ¼-tone pitch:

Thus ↑ can always be used in a sharpening context, ↓ always in a flattening context:

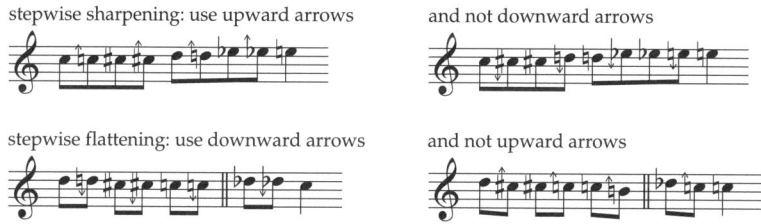

The correct enharmonic equivalents make reading much easier:

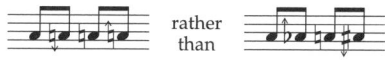

(See also *Note-spelling*, p. 85.)

There can be confusion as to whether an arrow defines an accidental as a ¼-tone or ¾-tone sharp or flat. The arrow modifies the given accidental by a ¼-tone in the direction of the arrow:

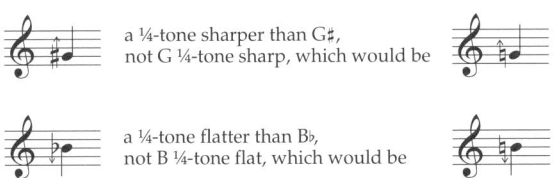

Using fixed symbols

The following are 'fixed symbols' in that they cannot modify a conventional accidental – as arrows can. They are useful to define ¼-tones should arrows be used to define another microtone in the same piece (see *Other microtones*, below).

The most commonly used symbols are:

The sharp symbols are especially easy to memorize as they look exactly like the degrees of sharpening that they represent. Signs used for a ¼-tone flat that should be avoided are: ↓ and ♭↓, ♭ and ♭♭ since these symbols are too similar to the flat sign. It is recommended that all four of the above fixed symbols are used (rather than exclusively sharp symbols, for instance) so that sharp symbols can be used in 'sharpening' contexts and flat symbols in 'flattening' ones.

Other microtones

Since there are no standard symbols, individual ones must be created for microtones other than ¼-tones.

The best symbols are those designed to be placed in front of a pitch, as this is the conventional position for accidentals – and not above the note. (Numerals to define microtones placed above the stave can look like fingering, and arrows above a stave appear to indicate playing direction of arpeggiated chords for stringed instruments.)

The most successful symbols are modified conventional accidentals, since such signs are immediately recognizable as pitch adjustment. Use arrows in the first instance (see *Arrow definition*, opposite).

Symbols should be as compact as possible. The further the symbol is from the note, the more difficult the pitch is to read. Wide symbols force short durations apart, which is unhelpful:

(In this example, ↑ and + might be defined as, say, 'raise pitch by a sixth of a tone', double symbols as 'raise pitch by a third of a tone'.)

Where possible, symbols should be attached to an accidental. Otherwise they may precede or supersede an accidental (but always in front of the note).

Make symbols as simple as possible so that they are legible on the stave. They should be easily distinguishable from other accidentals and from each other. For example, in *Medea-senecae*, the ⅓-tone symbols that Xenakis uses: ¢ = ⅓-tone higher, ¢ = ⅔-tone higher, contrast well with the ¼-tone notation ⸸ and ♯ (¾-tone).

Xenakis: *Medea-senecae*

Arrow definition

An arrow may be used to notate microtones other than the ¼-tone. The pitch modification of the arrow must always be defined. Arrows will represent one of the following definitions:

- Modify the pitch by a single given interval (e.g. of ⅓-, ⅕-, ⅙-tone, etc.)
- Modify the pitch within a given interval (e.g. by up to ¼-tone; between ⅛ and ¼-tone)
- Modify the pitch slightly

Arrows should have one meaning only in a piece. Introduce a second symbol if there are two different divisions of the tone (e.g. ⅓- and ¼-tones).

Cancelling microtonal alteration

If using conventional accidental practice, an ordinary accidental must cancel a microtone (the second and fourth notes in the second example remain microtonally altered):

4
Dynamics and Articulation

CONTENTS

DYNAMICS 101

ARTICULATION 109

Slurs 109

Articulation marks 114

Dynamics

Typography

All wording referring to dynamics uses an italic typeface. A stylized bold italic gives symbols *p*, *f*, *m*, *s* and *z* an individual and weighty appearance. No other text with the music should be as conspicuous. Relative to the stave, the *f* is 2½ stave-spaces high, the *p* is 2 spaces. The *m* (as in *mezzo*), *s* and *z* (as in *sf* and *fz*) are the height of a stave-space. Other wording for dynamics such as *cresc.*, *dim.*, *sempre*, is the same size and should use lower-case italic but never a bold typeface.

General conventions for placing dynamics

Place dynamics below the stave for instruments that use only a single stave.

All parts on one stave are assumed to have a common dynamic (placed below the stave) unless otherwise specified. This is regardless of whether the parts are stemmed together or separately. When parts sharing a stave have individual dynamics, each part must take separate stems. Dynamics for the up-stemmed part are then placed above the stave (see following section).

For vocal music, dynamics go above the stave to avoid conflict with the text.

For braced parts (keyboard and harp), dynamics usually go between the two staves, except where an individual hand or line requires its own dynamics. In this case, dynamics are usually best placed below each stave. The overriding consideration should be that dynamics are as close as possible to the part to which they apply.

In a score, two adjacent staves of the same instrumental family may share a line of dynamics, centred between the two staves, the sharing indicated with a brace { .

(For placing dynamics with grace notes, see *Dynamics*, p. 130.)

Placing dynamics relative to the stave

Dynamics should always be placed as close as possible to the notes to which they refer so that they cannot be overlooked. However, other markings – such as those for articulation, slurs, octave signs and tuplet brackets – are required to be closer to notes, so add these markings to the music before positioning dynamics:

(See also *Horizontal alignment*, p. 105.)

Hairpins (< >) should never intersect a stave-line, although this occasionally occurs in keyboard writing. In such a case, the hairpin must take a sufficiently steep slant to distinguish it from the stave-lines. A dynamic or hairpin placed on the stave becomes inconspicuous – at worst illegible.

Under exceptional conditions, a dynamic marking may be allowed to encroach into the outer stave-spaces, e.g. to minimize vertical space requirements in a large full score. This is also permissible in choral music, to prevent the dynamic colliding with the text of a voice part above:

When a middle voice requires a separate dynamic, this must be placed beside its notehead:

Note that in order to be legible, the bowl of *p* must intersect a line (and not sit in a space); the crossbar of *f* must not fall on a line.

VERTICAL ALIGNMENT OF DYNAMIC SYMBOLS

Centre the dynamic on the notehead:

When a closely following note takes a different dynamic, three or more characters (e.g. ***ppp***) move to the left so that the last character aligns with the notehead:

(See also *Breaking a barline for a dynamic*, below.)

When vertical space is limited, move a dynamic to the left of the note – never to the right, since the note has already started:

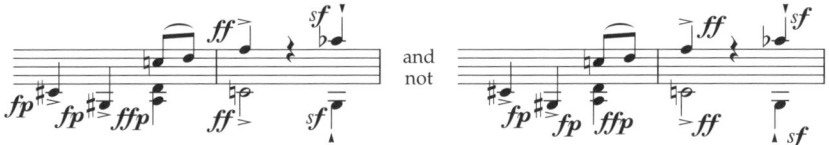

BREAKING A BARLINE FOR A DYNAMIC

It is acceptable to have a break in a barline for text such as technical instructions and expression marks and for dynamic symbols (but not for hairpins – see *Through barlines*, p. 105). However, it is always best to have continuous barlines if markings can be moved before or after the barline.

Move an initial dynamic to the right of a barline if possible. Make a break in a barline for a dynamic that cannot move right:

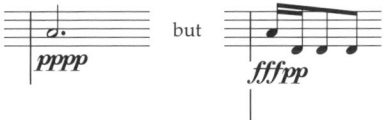

Crescendo/diminuendo signs (Hairpins)

Hairpins are the thickness of a stave-line. The open end should not be more than two stave-spaces wide. The open ends of complementary hairpins should match in width, and align horizontally:

$f <>$ $p < \quad > p$ and not $p < \quad > p$

The intensity of a dynamic change is not reflected by the openness of a hairpin, which maintains the same width regardless of dynamic:

$p < mp < ff > p$

(See also *Using crescendo/diminuendo signs or text*, p. 106.)

EXTENDING OVER A SYSTEM BREAK

A diminuendo hairpin remains open at the end of a system; a crescendo hairpin is left open at the beginning of the new system. A hairpin stops with the final barline and begins with the first note of the new system (or just before):

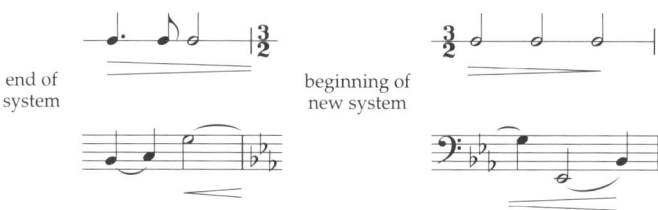

HORIZONTAL PLACING

A hairpin will always be a very precise length: this is its great advantage. Therefore it must be carefully placed or its significance will change:

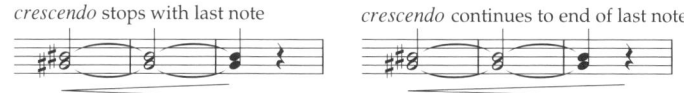

Do not place a hairpin before a note is started, nor after a note is finished. A hairpin should start at the first relevant notehead (not accidental) and end with the following notehead or at the first rest thereafter. Good practice is to start the hairpin on the left-hand edge of the note and to finish it on the right-hand edge of a note:

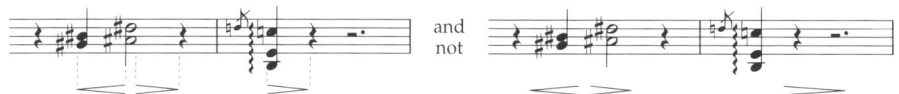

(If a dynamic symbol is present, the hairpin starts later and finishes earlier, so that the dynamic centres on the notehead or chord.)

When precision is important, subdivide note-values so that dynamics can be placed precisely:

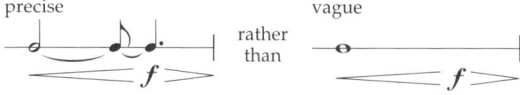

THROUGH BARLINES

A hairpin may cut through a barline, but should not start nor finish on a barline. It is neatest if a hairpin that terminates at the beginning of a bar stops short of the barline, since the space between the barline and the subsequent first beat has no time value (bars 1–3). However, it is helpful to extend a hairpin to a first beat that is some distance after a barline, to show continuity (bars 4–6):

HORIZONTAL ALIGNMENT

When a sequence of changing dynamics involves hairpins, keep such markings on the same horizontal plane whenever possible. The eye most easily follows a progression of dynamics running parallel to the stave:

It is sometimes necessary to tilt hairpins (as in the example below) so that they will fit into a vertically compact score.

In performance material, for clarity, it is important to keep dynamics as close as possible to the notes to which they refer. A hairpin may slope to follow the contour of the pitches, so that it visibly relates to its beginning and ending dynamics (where these are present). Avoid steep gradients if possible:

A sequence of dynamics at different vertical positions should be avoided as the dynamics will appear unconnected and be difficult to follow:

incorrect

Using crescendo/diminuendo signs or text

Use hairpins rather than words for a short crescendo or diminuendo, as they are quicker to read and are more conspicuous. However, long hairpins confuse the eye, as the long lines are virtually parallel to the stave. Instead, use the terms *crescendo* (abbrev. *cresc.*), *diminuendo* (abbrev. *dim.*) or *decrescendo* (abbrev. *decresc.*).

Widely spaced dashes or dots following on from these indications may be used to identify the duration of the dynamic change – usually to a specified final dynamic (the following example would be stretched over several bars):

cresc. _ _ _ *f*   or   *cresc.* _ _ *al* _ _ *f*

A reminder in brackets (*cresc.*)/(*dim.*) is useful at the beginning of a new system.

Qualifying dynamic change

VERBAL QUALIFICATION

Terms such as *poco a poco*, *più*, *molto* and *meno* alert the reader to:

- a gradual change over a long passage (e.g. *cresc. poco a poco*)
- a sudden change (e.g. *dim. molto*)
- a change from a preceding pattern:

Qualifying text should be placed above or below a hairpin – to place text inside a hairpin obscures the text or opens up the hairpin too much:

p ⎯⎯ *ppp*   but   *p* ⎯*poco*⎯   *molto*⎯ *ppp*   nor   *p* ⎯*poco*⎯   *molto*⎯ *ppp*
  poco   *molto*   not

Qualifying text occurring before or after a hairpin is ambiguous as it appears to refer to the starting or finishing dynamic:

incorrect
p poco ⎯⎯ *molto* ⎯⎯

INTERIM DYNAMICS

Dynamics may be added at strategic points during a long crescendo or diminuendo, e.g. for a new phrase or after rests. This is a precautionary measure to advise the performer not to change the dynamic level too quickly or too slowly. Interim dynamics should be used sparingly: their repeated use can look fussy and destroy the impression of a long phrase. Alternatively, add reminders such as *cresc./dim. sempre* after rests or at the beginning of a new system.

Place interim dynamics in brackets, to indicate their transitional status:

A hairpin may be broken for an interim dynamic. Maintain the same angle for the hairpin either side of the interim dynamic, so that the hairpin is clearly one gradual dynamic change. It is unnecessary in this case to enclose the interim dynamic in brackets since it is clear that the dynamic change continues:

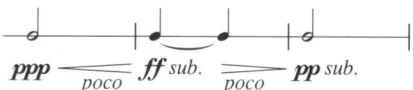

SUDDEN DYNAMIC CHANGES

The term *subito* ('suddenly'; abbrev. *sub.*) alerts the performer to an abrupt dynamic change. It also indicates that an interim dynamic change has not been omitted.

Use *subito* to show when a dynamic is not the logical conclusion of a hairpin:

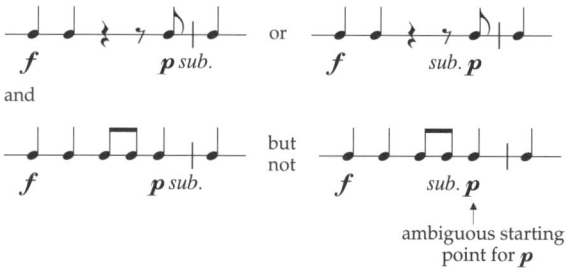

Place a dynamic exactly under the first note to which it refers, and fit in *sub.* around the dynamic: usually to the right, so that the placing of the new dynamic is not ambiguous. When a rest precedes the dynamic, *sub.* may also precede the dynamic:

Where there is not space to include *sub.*, use a vertical stroke or dotted line between each sudden dynamic change:

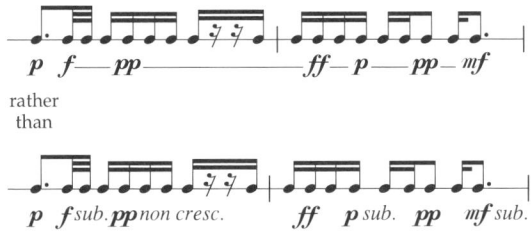

A dynamic may be followed by a horizontal line to indicate no dynamic change (e.g. when another part does take a change of dynamic). This makes cautionary *non cresc.*/*non dim.* instructions and the use of *subito* redundant:

Niente

Niente = nothing; *dim. al niente* = fade to nothing

A small circle at the closed end of a hairpin may be used to indicate growing from, as well as fading to, nothing. The circle is best attached to the hairpin, since a free-floating circle is inconspicuous:

Not every performer will be conversant with this notation, and so it should be clarified with an explanatory note.

Repetition of dynamics

In ensemble music, reiterate dynamics after rests, to save the performer looking back for a dynamic while preparing for the next entry. 'Reminder' dynamics may be given in ordinary round brackets (as in the first example under *Interim dynamics*, p. 107). The brackets indicate an unchanged dynamic. These are useful especially when other performers have different dynamic levels. But it is not helpful to reiterate an unchanged dynamic constantly, since this tends to clutter the music.

A repeated pattern of dynamics should always be written out in full rather than using *simile* or *sim.* (as is customary for repeated articulation: see *Repeated articulation*, p. 116). The performer will almost certainly forget them completely:

(For *sforzando* and *rinforzando*, see *Intensity of attack*, p. 115.)

Articulation

Slurs

The slur has a number of different meanings relating to articulation in addition to its general use as a phrase mark. For the wind player, it is the number of notes not separately tongued; for the string player, the number of notes in a bow stroke; for the singer, the number of notes sung to one syllable (and known as the syllabic slur).

Design

The slur is the same tapered arc as the tie, although the tie may have a flatter curve to allow room for slurs and to differentiate the two (see *Ties*, p. 60). When notes at the beginning and end of a slur are the same pitch, the slur may look identical to a tie because it will, like the tie, be completely symmetrical. When the outer pitches are different, the ends of the slur are at different heights and the slur tilts between the first and last note. Aim for as consistent a curve as possible:

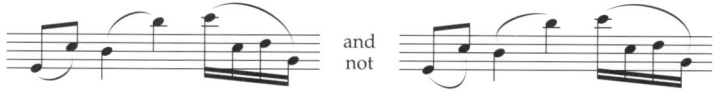

The curve of a long slur is flattened in order to be as close to the stave as possible. In fact, a long slur may be completely flat in the middle, since a rounded one extends too far from the stave:

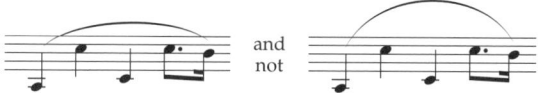

On a stave, the arc should be placed in a stave-space in order to be most conspicuous:

Positioning relative to the stave

When all stems within the slur are in the same direction, the slur is usually placed between the outer noteheads.

When groups of mixed stem direction are encompassed by a slur, place the slur above the stave, except when a beam may be in the way:

Regardless of stem direction, in cramped conditions it may sometimes be best to place a long slur above the stave, to be clear of dynamics:

Slurs for the left-hand stave of a keyboard part may go below the stave to be clear of mid-system dynamics.

For stemless notes, place the slur as if the notes were stemmed (a). Slurs for notes on the centre line and chords equidistant from the centre line can go either side, but are usually treated as if the notes had down-stems (b):

Positioning relative to noteheads and stems

SLURS NEXT TO NOTEHEADS

The ends of a slur may be placed as close as half a stave-space from the centre of noteheads, including where ties are placed at the edge of noteheads (a). Where there is plenty of space, the tie starts and finishes at the centre of the notehead; in this case, the slur must move further from the note, so that its ends can also centre on it (b):

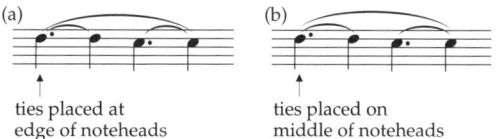

(See also *Placing articulation and slurs with ties*, p. 62.)

SLURS AT STEM END

Where other notes or stems will not be obstructed, the slur may move slightly closer to the noteheads, beside the stems, so as to be more conspicuous:

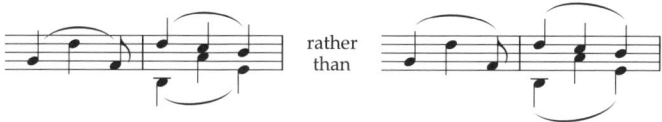

Where staccato and tenuto marks falls within the slur, the slur cannot move towards the noteheads but must remain at the ends of the stems:

(See *Placing slurs with other articulation marks*, p. 121.)

When outer notes have opposite stem directions, move the slur at the stem end towards the noteheads so it does not tilt contrary to the direction of the pitches:

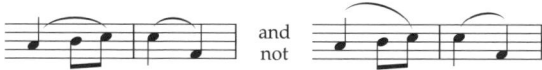

The slur should not, however, move too close to noteheads if there is room for it to be further away. It should always remain outside a beam:

Slurs over a system break

At the end of a system, the slur finishes just short of the last barline, and not beyond it. At the beginning of the new system, the slur starts after the clef, key signature and time signature, but before any accidental. The incomplete slur should look clearly open-ended, or each side of the system break will appear to take a separate slur:

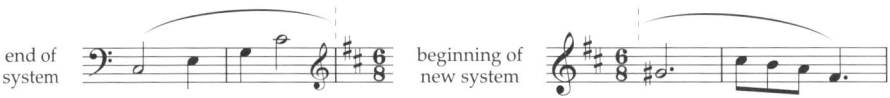

Take all the notes within the slur into account when determining whether the slur goes above or below the stave – do not swap position between systems:

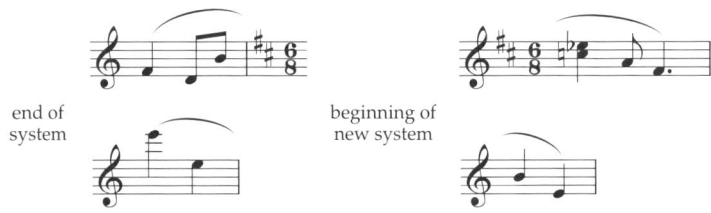

The whole slur should tilt in the direction of the pitches (as in the second example above). A slur starting on the last note of a system or finishing on the first note of a system must be angled in the direction of the final pitch on the new system, so as to look clearly open-ended (this differentiates an open-ended slur from an open-ended tie):

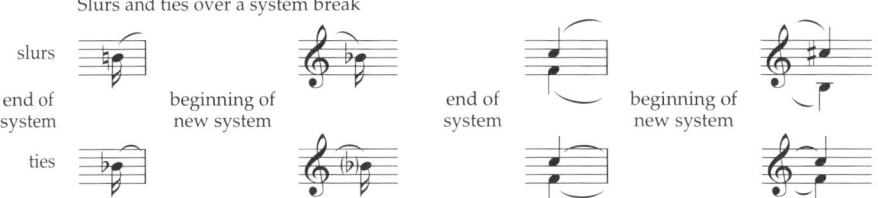

Slur length

One complete slur should cover a whole phrase, so that its full extent is immediately clear. Do not divide a slur between notes of a phrase, nor around tied notes. In full scores, divided phrase marks are sometimes used in cramped conditions, to save space. These should never be used in performance material, since they obscure the phrase length:

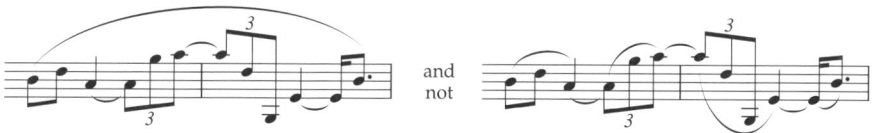

When a final pitch is extended by a series of tied notes, it is acceptable (and a convention) to end the slur with the first whole-bar duration (a); alternatively, in cramped conditions, with the first tied note (b):

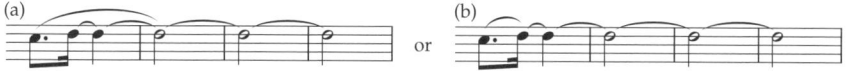

When an initial note is tied, the slur may begin with the final written tied note if absolutely necessary, to save space; however, it is much better to clarify phrase length by starting the slur with the first note:

Slurs within slurs

When two slurs are used simultaneously, the shorter one represents articulation, the longer one the phrase structure. The shorter slur goes closest to the notes:

Note that it is best not to use two sets of slurs in music for wind and strings, since this causes confusion (see also *Two-note tremolos: Slurs*, p. 228).

Dotted slurs

A dotted slur may indicate where a literal legato is not possible, i.e. where individual notes within a phrase are rearticulated:

When a phrase includes rests, a solid slur is equally valid, and visually less fussy:

Slurs between chords

All notes on one stem take a single slur, and not a slur to each note:

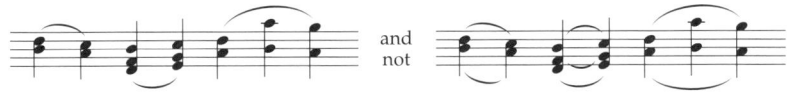

For adjacent-note chords, centre the slur on the notehead that is on the correct side of the stem:

(For combining slurs and ties between chords, see *With slurs*, p. 71.)

If parts are separately stemmed, each requires its own slurs (see *In double-stemmed writing*, p. 117).

(See also *Placing slurs with other articulation marks*, p. 121; for placing slurs with grace notes, see *Slurs*, p. 129.)

Articulation marks

Definition

Articulation marks are interpreted by their context – the style and period of the music. They have the flexibility to be adapted to different styles; conversely, this can lend them an ambiguity to challenge the interpreter. Since different schools of performance may assume separate interpretations, it can be advisable to state at the beginning of a piece exactly how articulation should be performed, especially if interpretation is to differ from the definition given opposite.

In general, present-day interpretation is as follows:

ARTICULATION MARKS

𝅘𝅥 (with ^) strong accent (see also *Intensity of attack*, below)

𝅘𝅥 (with >) standard accent

𝅘𝅥 (with —) tenuto: separated articulation, or a stress, or a note held for its full duration

𝅘𝅥 (with wedge) staccato wedge or dash: a heavy staccato (between marcato and staccato), also *staccatissimo* (see below)

𝅘𝅥 (with dot) staccato (abbrev. *stacc.*)

Staccatissimo (abbrev. *staccatiss.*) is best indicated verbally together with staccato dots.

The tenuto line 𝅘𝅥 implies either holding a note for its full length, or a slight separation from surrounding notes: 𝅘𝅥 𝅘𝅥 𝅘𝅥. In combination with a staccato mark it lengthens the note: 𝅘𝅥 and 𝅘𝅥.

INTENSITY OF ATTACK

The accent symbols above may be replaced by the following terms:

- *sforzando / sforzato* ('reinforcing'; both abbrev. *sf* or *sfz*) is used for a sudden accent
- *rinforzando / rinforzato* (abbrev. *rf / rfz / rinf.*) has the same meaning but is sometimes used for a part (or a passage) that should predominate

These terms can be modified according to the dynamic: at dynamic levels of *f* they appear as *sf* or *sfz*, at *ff*, they become *sff* or *sffz*; and at *fff*, *sfff* or *sfffz*.

STRESS SYMBOLS INTRODUCED BY SCHOENBERG

Schoenberg introduced symbols to represent a stressed note: 𝅘𝅥 𝅘𝅥 and an unstressed note: 𝅘𝅥 𝅘𝅥. These symbols function to indicate when stresses contradict the metre (see *Cross rhythm*, p. 171).

The symbols should be placed above the stave, except in double-stemmed writing (see bar 2), and outside any articulation marks:

Repeated articulation

Staccato sempre and *marcato sempre* indicate repeated articulation. It is helpful to notate the articulation in full initially:

Simile (abbrev. *sim.*) may replace repeated bars of other articulation marks, and combined marks:

(For articulation on repeated-note abbreviations, see *Repeated articulation*, p. 223.)

Symbol design

With the exception of the staccato dot, articulation marks should match the width and height of a notehead, or be slightly larger.

The strong accent ∧ : this is thicker on one side than the other: ∧ ∨. The up-bow symbol ⋁, which has two thin diagonal strokes, is not a substitute.

The standard accent > : this has lines of equal thickness. It is slightly wider than a notehead, but if it is too wide it may look like a diminuendo hairpin:

and
not

The tenuto line: this is thicker than a stave-line so as to be conspicuous. It is the width of a notehead.

The staccato wedge: this sign should be sufficiently bold for it to be easily distinguished from a staccato dot:

The staccato dot: this is smaller than the duration dot:

Placing articulation next to noteheads or stems

Articulation goes where it is most conspicuous: to the notehead. Except in double-stemmed writing (see below), never place articulation below down-stems:

(For placing articulation on grace notes, see *Articulation*, p. 130.)

The strong accent ʌ usually goes above the stave, regardless of stem direction, because of the amount of space it occupies. Placing the accent above the stave also avoids its inversion ᴠ, which, in some contexts, may look like an up-bow symbol in string writing:

When space below the stave is limited, all articulation may be placed above:

In double-stemmed writing

Each part requires its own articulation marks (including slurs), even when the two parts have identical articulation and phrasing. This includes unisons:

Place articulation marks at the end of each stem. Articulation should never be placed on the notehead side of a part as it must be clear which marking belongs to which note. Any articulation on the stave is extremely confusing in double-stemmed writing:

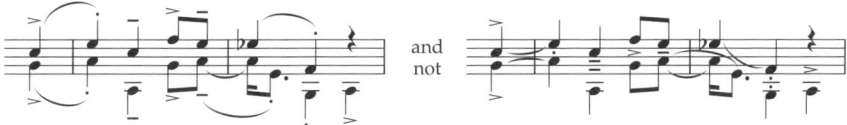

Articulation should not move closer to the note than the end of the stem, as this also is confusing:

(See also *Placing slurs with other articulation marks*, p. 121.)

Exact positioning beside noteheads and stems

Articulation is centred in line with the notehead, whether positioned next to a notehead or a stem (but see also *Staccatos at stem end*, below):

Thus, in double-stemmed writing, the articulation aligns vertically between the parts. (Some editions do, however, centre articulation on the stem.)

STACCATOS AT STEM END

Staccato dots and wedges by themselves look best centred on a stem and therefore are an exception to the above rule (see (a) below), although many editions do centre them on the notehead (b). They may move beside the stem in cramped conditions (c):

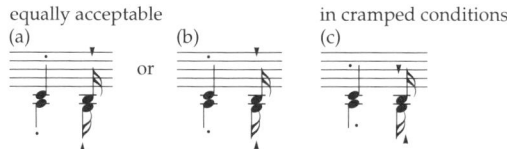

When staccato dots or wedges are combined with other articulation marks – which are always centred on the notehead – staccato dots should be centred too:

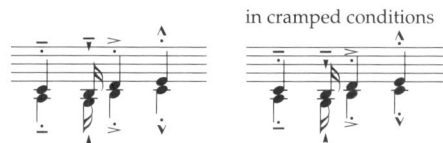

STEMLESS NOTES

Place articulation as if the note were stemmed. Notes on the centre line or chords equidistant from the centre line are usually treated as if they had down-stems (bar 3):

When there are two parts on one stave, articulation for stemless notes moves in close to the noteheads:

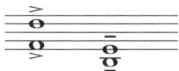

ADJACENT- AND UNISON-NOTE CHORDS

Centre articulation on the notehead that is on the correct side of the stem:

Distance from noteheads

Articulation marks are best placed a consistent distance from each notehead, so that the eye can follow them most easily:

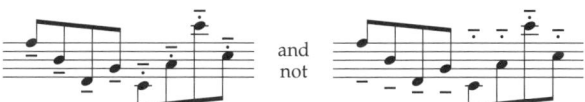

ARTICULATION ON THE STAVE

Place articulation marks no closer than the first clear stave-space from the note.

Centre tenuto lines and staccato dots in a stave-space:

notes in a space:
placed in the space next to the note

notes on a line:
placed in the next clear space

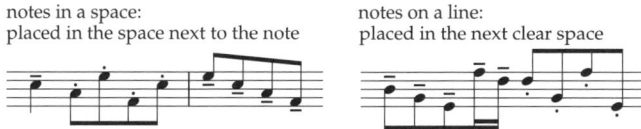

A stave-line must never obscure the articulation:

Accents > ʌ and staccato wedges are usually best placed outside the stave, where they are most conspicuous. They can move onto the stave when they would otherwise be a long way from the note (see following two examples).

The accent > is clearest when centred in a space. As it tends to obscure a pitch when placed in the stave, a series of accents is best placed outside the stave:

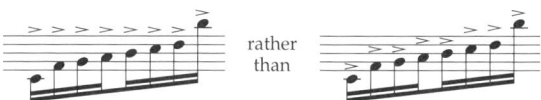

The ʌ accent and staccato wedge should intersect a stave-line for greatest legibility. The top part of the ʌ accent intersects the line so that the white space at the peak shows through:

An additional mark takes a separate stave-space further from the note. Do not cram more than one articulation mark into a stave-space or both become illegible:

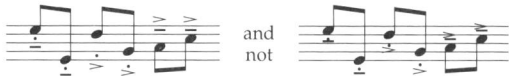

When ledger-line notes require articulation between the notehead and the stave, place articulation marks no closer to the notes than the outermost stave-spaces. This ensures that articulation does not collide nor obscure ledger lines:

Tenuto lines should be even further from ledger lines (b) so that the eye does not confuse the two (c). When there are several notes on ledger lines, tenuto lines are best placed at the stem ends of up-stemmed notes, for clarity (a):

Distance from stems

Within the stave, place articulation marks in the first clear stave-space beyond the end of the stem. Articulation outside the stave should be about half a stave-space from each stem:

Only staccato dots and wedges may fall within the length of the stem (see *Staccatos at stem end*, p. 118).

Placing slurs with other articulation marks

The smallest signs go closest to the notehead:

The staccato wedge is placed in the same position as the staccato dot.

Usually, only tenuto lines and staccato marks may go inside the first and last notes of a slur:

(See also *Interpreting tenuto and staccato marks at ends of slurs*, p. 122.)

Articulation marks in the middle of a slur go inside the slur. Accents at the beginning and end of a slur usually go outside the slur, so that the slur can remain closer to the noteheads:

An exception is when they would otherwise be too far from a note to be immediately apparent:

When notes within a slur have mixed stem direction, place articulation marks beside each notehead, even though the slur is above the stave:

Centre a slur on a stem. With the addition of a tenuto line between the slur and a stem, centre the slur, like the tenuto line, on the notehead (when there is a staccato dot, the slur centres on the stem):

INTERPRETING TENUTO AND STACCATO MARKS AT ENDS OF SLURS

To show a slur between two consecutive notes of the same pitch, place articulation between slur and noteheads:

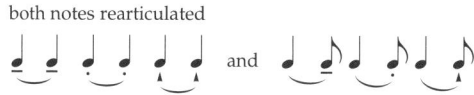

When articulation is placed outside the slur on either or both of the two notes, the slur becomes a tie:

5

*Grace Notes,
Arpeggiated Chords, Trills,
Glissandos and Vibrato*

Grace notes 125

Arpeggiated chords 131

Trills 134

Glissandos 140

Vibrato 146

Grace notes

Design

Grace notes are notated as small noteheads with stems shortened to about 2¼ stave-spaces. Tails, beams, articulation and accidentals are also scaled down proportionally. The sharp and natural signs become 2 spaces long (rather than the normal 3), the flat is 1¾ spaces long.

The grace note is slightly smaller than a cue note, which is ¾ of a full-sized note.

A single grace note is a small quaver with a diagonal stroke that intersects the tail. It is essential to use the diagonal stroke to differentiate the grace note from an appoggiatura:

A group of grace notes is joined by one or more beams. A diagonal stroke may be placed through the beam if grace notes might otherwise be confused with an appoggiatura.

The traditional practice is to use most commonly two, but often three, beams to join groups of two or more notes. Two beams are recommended as they give the least cluttered appearance:

Some editions use two beams to join two notes and three beams to join three or more notes. Four beams sometimes join four or more notes:

It is common practice to place a diagonal line through a single beam. If preferred, in addition two or more beams may be used (as above):

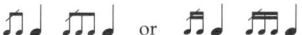

The diagonal line should intersect the tail or beam without colliding with the notehead:

Ensure that a grace note on ledger lines has a sufficiently long stem for the diagonal stroke not to obscure a ledger line:

(See also *Ledger lines*, p. 26.)

Place the diagonal stroke so that, ideally, white space shows through between the stem, the tail or beam and the diagonal.

PLACING DIAGONAL LINES ON GRACE-NOTE GROUPS

Place the line at the beginning of a group, and diagonally to the beam:

With double-stemmed beams (stems extending in both directions from a beam), the stem direction of the first note determines the position of the diagonal line. The direction of the diagonal is the same as for the single grace note of the same stem direction:

Stem direction

Grace notes take up-stems, regardless of their position on the stave. An exception to this is where there are two parts on one stave, in which case the lower part takes down-stems:

The other exceptions are: where there are double-stemmed beams (as shown above); also, where grace notes are attached to a measured value (see *Grace notes on the beat*, p. 129).

Alignment

RELATIVE TO THE BARLINE

Grace notes are placed before the position of the beat regardless of whether they are performed on or before the beat. Grace notes preceding the first beat of a bar are usually placed after the barline:

Grace notes sounding on the beat should always be placed after the barline. However, a group of three or more grace notes sounding before the beat may go before the barline so that the first beat of the following bar is not pushed too far from the barline:

(See also *Performing grace notes on or before the beat*, p. 128.)

The finishing notes of a trill or tremolo are written as grace notes and should be placed before the barline:

(See *Trills: Starting and finishing notes*, p. 138.)

RELATIVE TO ANOTHER PART

Grace notes written after the barline displace the first beat to the right. All other parts align with the measured value and not with the grace notes (see following example).

In a score, when grace-note groups come after the beginning of the bar, note-spacing in one part need not necessarily be expanded to accommodate grace notes in another part, even though the grace notes start later in the bar than the rhythmic alignment suggests. This facilitates score-reading, as it prevents distorted note-spacing of a single beat:

Observe correct vertical alignment in a single-instrument part, so as not to confuse the player:

When there are two parts on one stave, align the grace notes of the two parts:

When two parts with grace notes are on separate staves, it may be more helpful visually to close up grace notes to the following measured value, regardless of vertical alignment (accidentals may force some grace notes further apart than others and precise vertical alignment causes unwanted gaps between notes):

Performing grace notes on or before the beat

Unless the context is very obvious, clarify where grace notes are to be placed. To write grace notes before a barline clearly indicates that they should be sounded before the first beat but this notation is limited to first beats. A general instruction is unambiguous: 'all grace notes to be placed before the beat/on the beat'.

When grace notes are to be placed both on and before the beat, different articulation may indicate placing (clarify this with an instruction):

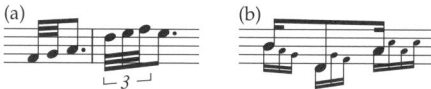

GRACE NOTES ON THE BEAT

If accents are not appropriate, differentiate notes to be sounded on the beat either by writing them in rhythm (a) or, alternatively, by joining them to a measured note (b). In the latter case, grace-note stems should point away from the measured notes:

Slurs

Grace notes are slurred to the following measured value, provided that this is the required articulation. In drum notation, a slur indicates a rebounding stroke played by the same hand. Consequently, it is incorrect to use a slur for a single grace note because the strokes are played with different hands.

The slur goes below the grace note, from notehead to notehead:

When there are two parts on a stave, curve the grace-note slurs away from the stave. The slurs may be placed close to noteheads where they would otherwise collide with beams (third beat):

A slur must not obscure a ledger line. It is often preferable to place slurs above ledger lines to avoid collision:

A slur should always be placed above the notes when it would otherwise collide with the accidentals of a measured value:

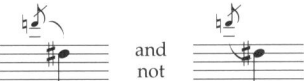

and so that grace notes can be slurred to the uppermost note of a chord (the slur should lead to the pitch that resolves the ornament):

It is usual (and recommended practice) for each grace-note group to take an independent slur, even when this occurs within a standard slur. Each independent slur helps to identify visually the grace-note groups:

It is also acceptable to include grace notes within a standard slur, and to omit independent slurs. Although this is less fussy, the grace notes lose some visual definition:

Articulation

Place articulation for grace notes where it will be most conspicuous – this will usually be outside the stave since scaled-down articulation is difficult to see on the stave:

Dynamics

Traditionally, a dynamic is centred under the measured value, except when grace notes take separate dynamics. It is also acceptable to place a dynamic under the first grace note. The longer the group of grace notes, the more useful it is to do this, as the dynamic is more conspicuous at the beginning of the group:

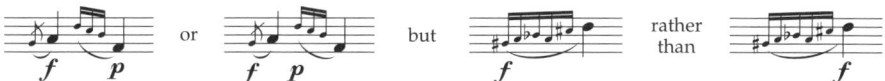

(See also *Accidentals affecting grace notes*, p. 84.)

Arpeggiated chords

Design

The arpeggio sign is a wavy line similar to, or the same as, the design of the shaded trill line (see *Extent of the trill line*, p. 136). This extends vertically to encompass all arpeggiated notes (but not the stems as well). The sign should precede any accidentals, and must come after a barline:

The arpeggio sign always precedes a chord. A wavy line placed after a chord (* above) is used by Bartók (e.g. in the 14 Bagatelles for piano, op. 6) to indicate a downward arpeggio (but see below for recommended notation).

Arpeggio direction

A chord is arpeggiated from bottom to top pitches unless otherwise indicated.

A chord arpeggiated from top to bottom takes a downward arrow:

A subsequent upward arpeggio requires an upward arrow:

An upward arrow is needed only when there are also downward arpeggios.

An arrow preceding the arpeggio sign has the same meaning, but occupies more space:

An arrow without a wavy line indicates a fast strum for various stringed instruments (harp, guitar and pizzicato bowed strings).

Extent of arpeggiation

Sempre arpeggiando (abbrev. *arpegg.* or *arp.*) or *arpeggiando sempre* indicates repeated arpeggiation. This may be used as a general instruction to replace the arpeggio sign (this is the norm in harp music), or as an instruction to continue arpeggiation after the initial use of the arpeggio sign (as is the norm in keyboard and guitar music).

Non-arpeggiated chords are then indicated *non arpeggiando* or, within an arpeggiated passage, by a vertical square bracket that encompasses the chord. When the chord is laid out across two staves, extend a single bracket across both staves. One bracket is quicker to read than individual brackets for each hand (although this is not incorrect) – see last bar:

CHORDS ARPEGGIATED ACROSS TWO STAVES

An unbroken arpeggio across two staves must be notated with one continuous line (as in the example above, bar 1).

A broken arpeggio, in which both hands arpeggiate simultaneously, has a separate arpeggio sign for each hand and, if included, an arrow for each sign. When both or either of the chords has accidentals, place each arpeggio sign as close to each chord as the accidentals will allow (the signs need not align between staves):

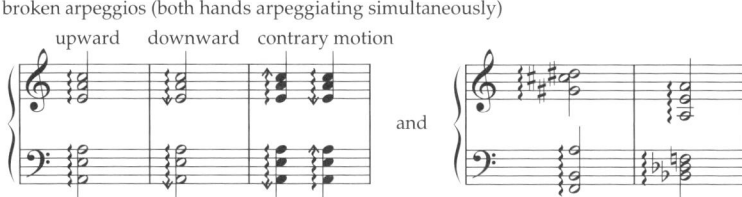

Changing dynamic during arpeggiation

A hairpin may be placed vertically through the stave(s), preceding the arpeggio sign, to cover the extent of the chord. Dynamics at either end of the hairpin are placed outside the stave:

Performing chords on or before the beat

A chord will be spread before the beat unless the playing style suggests otherwise. Chords spread on the beat should be indicated with a verbal instruction, e.g. 'All chords to be spread *on* the beat.' Alternatively, chords spread on the beat may be notated as consecutive pitches (see below).

Speed

The speed of arpeggiation should be prescribed verbally as *arpeggio lento / largo / rapido* or *slow / fast arpegg.*, and so on.

Arpeggiated chords notated as consecutive pitches

Slow arpeggios may be best notated as consecutive pitches, either as grace-note groups or in a given rhythm as appropriate.

An order of notes to be played other than directly up or down the chord should be notated as consecutive pitches (see example *Dividing ties*, below).

A notation convention allows consecutive notes joined by a beam to be tied over to a chord, even though this does not show accurate durations for every note (a). The double stems and durations of the following typical nineteenth-century example are unnecessary (b) as are the repeated tied notes of (c):

Should it not be possible to tie each note without obscuring a notehead, it is acceptable to divide one or more of the ties:

Tied notes must be reiterated across beats:

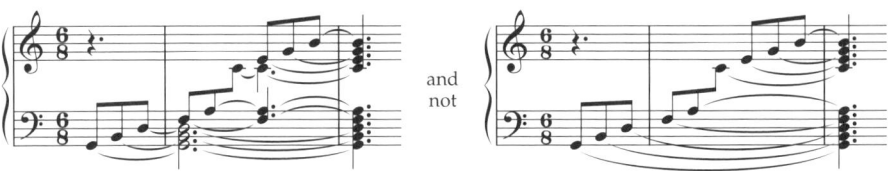

When notes are not held manually, *laissez vibrer* ties may be used instead (see *Laissez vibrer*, p. 72).

To release notes from a tied chord it is necessary to notate full durations for each tied note:

Trills

Definition

Although a trill is usually reserved to notate the alternation of notes a tone or semitone apart, the rapid alternation of any two notes, including a tremolo between two notes, may be notated as a trill.

In terms of performance practice, the starting note of the trill presupposes a prominence over the trilling note that is not implicit in a two-note tremolo. Some musicians feel that the trill has nineteenth-century performance-style connotations, and prefer the two-note tremolo notation. Either notation is equally valid.

Traditionally, the written note trills with its upper neighbouring note (a tone or semitone distant). However, it is acceptable to allow a trilling note to include wider (higher or lower) intervals. Thus a passage of alternating notes at different intervals may be notated either as trills:

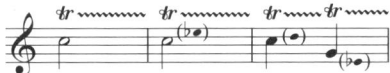

or as two-note tremolos:

rather than as a combination of the two, which looks disjointed:

(See also *Trilling note*, p. 138, and *Two-note tremolos*, p. 225.)

Design and placing

The trill (Italian: *trillo*) is represented by a stylized sign in bold italic: *tr* . The sign is always positioned above the stave except in double-stemmed writing. Place the sign flush with the left-hand edge of the notehead, further from the note than any articulation marks. Only a long slur, a pause or octave sign goes further from the stave.

DOUBLE TRILLS

In double-stemmed parts, the trill sign for the lower part goes below the stave. Where there is room, place any dynamic markings further from the stave:

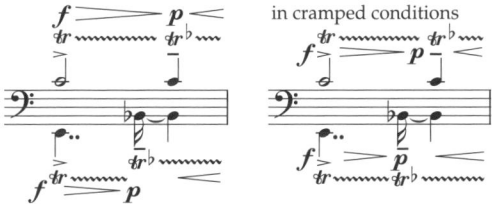

A single-stemmed chord comprising two instruments playing single trills or one instrument playing double trills may take single stems, as long as two trill signs are indicated. The signs may be placed each side of the chord, except where there is a third voice on the stave (see third example):

When one part only has a trill, assign the parts separate stems so that it is clear which part trills:

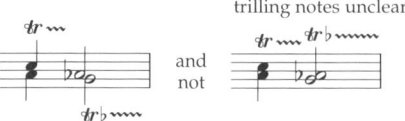

Extent of the trill line

The trill line – a shaded, wavy line, placed directly after the trill sign – is used to indicate the extent of a trill.

The trill line is optional for a single note-value, but must be used with tied notes (see also *Continuous or discontinuous trills*, opposite). The trill line extends for the entire duration of the note, and not merely as far as the last written note:

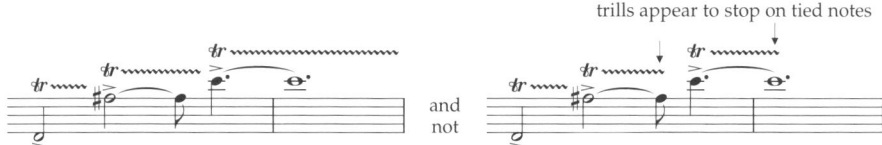

In the middle of a bar, the trill line continues right up to the following note-head or its accidental (if it has one):

The trill line stops at a barline:

At the end of a system, the trill line stops with the barline. (In score layout, the line stops just before the barline so as not to collide with it.)

When a trill is to terminate before the end of a note, divide the note-value to show the exact length of the trill. A tie indicates that the note following on from the trill is not re-articulated:

To indicate that the trill finishes before the next note, not with the next note, terminate the trill line with a vertical notch. Place the cut-off point before an accidental for the following note; at the end of a bar, place it on the barline:

TRILLS OVER A SYSTEM BREAK

The trill sign should, ideally, be repeated on a new system, above the first entry and in brackets, to indicate that the trill has already started. If brackets are not used, then the wavy line should precede the trill sign instead. A wavy line without a trill sign is sometimes used but this notation is less clear:

Continuous or discontinuous trills

For a continuous trill of more than one note-value, notes should be tied to indicate that there is no re-articulation on a following note. The trill line is continuous for the duration of the ties:

If a trill is to be re-articulated with each note-value, assign individual trill signs and omit ties:

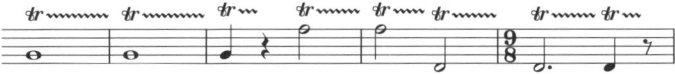

(The last example above is also the obsolete notation for continuous trills.)

Starting and finishing notes

A grace note may specify when the starting note is other than the written note (a). Grace notes should also be used to specify finishing notes. According to the required articulation, slur the grace notes to the measured note (b) or to the following note (c), or include both (d):

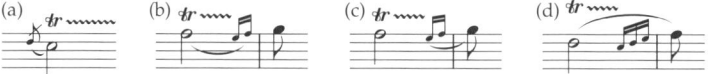

Trilling note

When no trilling note is indicated, it is the upper neighbouring note; this pitch is modified by a key signature. An accidental for the trilling note is either notated with an accidental sign alone, or with a written trilling note (see below).

WITH ACCIDENTAL SIGN ONLY

The accidental follows the trill sign or goes above it. Whichever layout is used depends on the priority for horizontal or vertical space-saving:

The accidental refers to the next note of the scale above the written note – not the same note of the scale:

To avoid any possible ambiguity, the trilling note may be written in (see below).

(See also *Accidentals affecting ornaments*, p. 84.)

WITH WRITTEN TRILLING NOTE

A trilling note that is the same note of the scale as the measured note (but with a different accidental) must be written in.

It is also necessary to notate a trilling note when it differs from a previous one (see example *Change of trilling note*, opposite).

Notate the trilling pitch as a small notehead in brackets after the measured note. Do not use a grace note for the trilling pitch; reserve grace notes for the starting and finishing notes of a trill (see *Starting and finishing notes*, opposite).

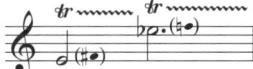

If the first note of a tied trill is a short value, add the trilling note after the second note, where there is more room. This avoids cramping or distorting the spacing of the short note:

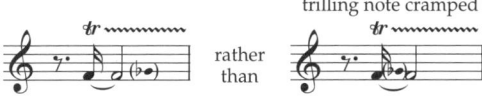

A tie should not run through a trilling note. It should start from the measured note if there is room; otherwise, after the trilling note:

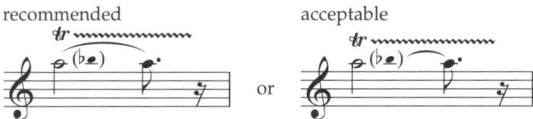

It is not necessary to indicate that the same trilling note continues over a barline or system break as this is assumed unless otherwise indicated. A change of trilling note is notated as follows:

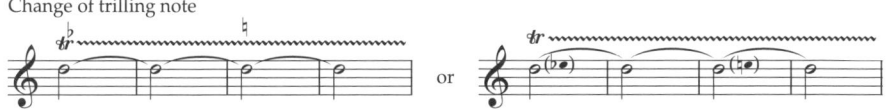

Variation in trill speed

This may be indicated by a verbal instruction above the trill line, as in the following example. In a complex score with many technical instructions, it may be helpful to change the intensity of the trill line itself, to reflect the changing speed, and thus a verbal instruction is necessary only in the first instance:

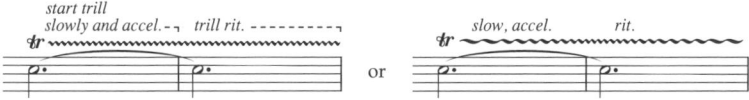

An alternative notation is to use a two-note tremolo with fanned beams (see *Beamed groups indicating variation in speed*, p. 158):

Glissandos

Definition

The term *glissando* (abbrev. *gliss.*) is used throughout this book as a generic term to describe both a chromatic-step scale between pitches, and a genuine microtonal slide covering all intermediary pitches.

Some schools of thought define *glissando* as 'to slide chromatically between pitches' (as on keyboard or harp). In practice, *glissando* frequently describes what has often been defined as a *portamento* (abbrev. *port.*): a smooth, microtonal slide, as can be produced on stringed instruments, trombone, and so on, and by voices.

The term *portamento* may, of course, be substituted in the following examples where appropriate. However, *port.* is often intended to indicate an expressive legato slide between two pitches, and the term *glissando* reserved for a more deliberate, continuous slide. (It is always safest to clarify intended interpretation in a preface.)

For instruments capable of producing both chromatic and microtonal glissandos (woodwind, brass and strings), it is necessary to clarify when only chromatic semitones are to be played. The chromatic pitches should be notated in full, as measured or grace notes. An instruction, *chromatic gliss.*, may be added for clarity.

A diagonal line indicates both glissando and portamento. A thin straight line is recommended, although some older editions use a wavy line (this can take up too much space):

The instructions *gliss.* or *port.* should also be placed close to the lines, and used at least at their first appearances. This is especially important in a part on two staves (keyboard and harp), so that the glissando line is not mistaken for a voice-leading indication (a solid or dotted line indicating the progression of a part that moves between two staves).

Placing the glissando line

The glissando line should follow the course of the pitches exactly. Angle it precisely between the noteheads (a). The line should not appear to start above the first notated pitch (b), nor to go beyond the finishing pitch (c):

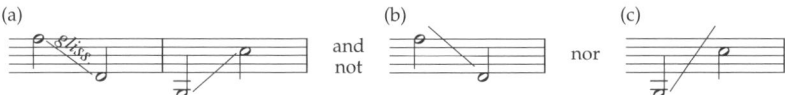

A glissando indication may be angled parallel to the line and be placed on the stave, as long as it remains legible ((a) above; see also double bass example, p. 13).

Shorten the length of a line only when the glissando is intentionally shorter than the interval between two pitches:

Where the distance between pitches is too short to contain a glissando line, place the line above or below the notes, away from the stems. In such cases, clarify the function of the line with a *gliss.* indication. Place the indication as close to the glissando line as possible:

When a repeated figure should no longer contain a glissando, the indication *non gliss.* is helpful (bar 2, above).

WITH ACCIDENTALS

A glissando line should not run through an accidental and risk obscuring it. Stop the line short of an accidental, or angle it to the left of the accidental:

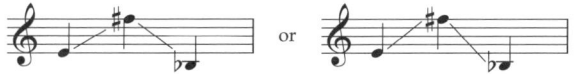

OVER A SYSTEM BREAK

Reflect the correct interval of a glissando in the gradient of the line:

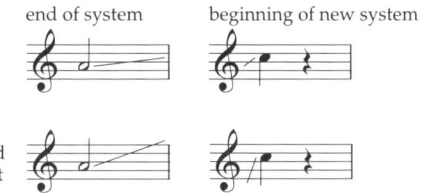

BETWEEN NOTES OF THE SAME PITCH LETTER

Angle a glissando line in the direction of the raised or lowered pitch, in order to illustrate the progression of the slide:

WITH CLEF CHANGES

Where possible, avoid changing clef in the course of a glissando: use ledger lines instead. The gradient of the line then reflects more clearly the intervals between pitches:

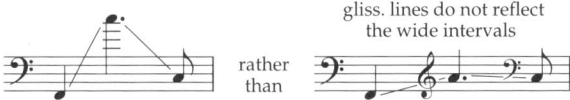

Never arrange a clef change so that the angle of the glissando line would be in the opposite direction to the slide:

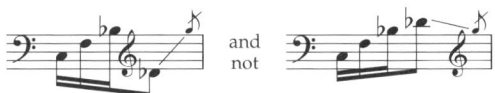

TO AND FROM UNSPECIFIED PITCHES

The glissando line should accurately reflect the intended pitch range. Do not give a steep gradient to a line that is likely to reflect only a small interval (see following example).

If the glissando is to an unspecified highest or lowest note, a triangular notehead indicates the end pitch of the glissando (see *Triangular noteheads*, p. 12):

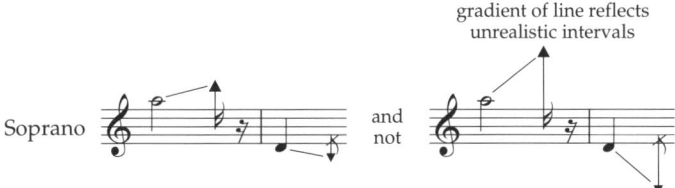

If the highest or lowest note available is a pitch that can be prescribed, notate this pitch rather than using a triangular notehead (see also *Finishing pitch*, p. 144).

In harp music, an arrow placed at the end of a glissando line indicates direction but not a specific finishing pitch.

The speed of a glissando to or from an unspecified pitch (as in the examples above) should be prescribed verbally, e.g. *gliss. rapido/lentiss.* or *fast/very slow gliss.*, since there cannot be a prescribed interval that would indicate how fast to cover the given duration.

PARALLEL GLISSANDOS

Place parallel lines for parallel glissandos. Each note of the chord must take a separate glissando line. Regardless of the number of notes, only one *gliss.* instruction is necessary:

WITH CLUSTERS

It is not practical to allocate separate glissando lines for individual pitches of a chromatic cluster (e.g. for keyboard). Instead, place a broad band to match the width of the cluster. The band may rise or fall as required:

Alternatively, if more practical, draw a glissando line for the outer pitches and fill in the band with shading (see Stockhausen, *Klavierstück X*).

Glissando starting midway through a duration

Divide an initial note-value to show exactly where a glissando starts:

When the exact starting point of a glissando is unspecified, an initial note-value need not be divided (a). To place a glissando just before the next measured value, tie the initial note to a grace note (b):

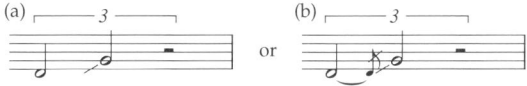

Finishing pitch

It is necessary to indicate an independent finishing pitch when a glissando is followed by a rest, by a separately articulated note or by a note that is other than the final pitch of the glissando (as in the following example). Notate the finishing pitch as a grace note or small stemless notehead. To indicate that the finishing pitch is not separately articulated, place a bracket around it (a) or add a slur between the two pitches (b):

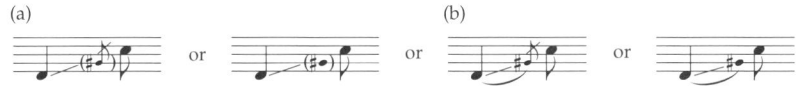

When the finishing note is to be separately articulated, clarify this by giving an articulation mark to the grace note:

Interim pitches

To indicate the progression of a slow or a long glissando, notate interim pitches in brackets either as small noteheads, or as note-values of the correct durations for the part of the bar in which they occur:

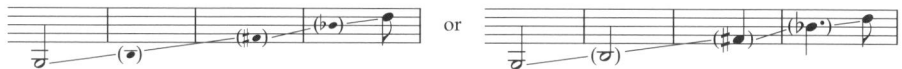

Note-value of initial pitch

The initial pitch should take the full duration of the glissando if this is possible within one note-value (a short note-value is not recommended, as it gives no clue of the glissando's duration):

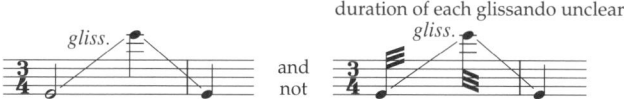

When the initial pitch cannot take full duration, it should take the longest duration it can: the value of a bar, half-bar or beat. Subsequent durations are indicated as outlined below.

Durations of more than one note-value

Notate the first note of the glissando as an ordinary note-value (see previous section). Subsequent note-values of less than a minim lose their noteheads but indicate their rhythms with stems close to or attached to the glissando line. Place any duration dot beside the stem, on the stem side of the glissando line. The direction of the stems is conventional, as if there were a notehead at the point where the glissando line intersects the stave. Since a bar looks incomplete or confusing without the notation of its total duration, indicate minims and semibreves as small note-values – with or without brackets – over the stave:

It is best not to notate all values subsequent to the initial pitch as small notes above the stave, since the eye has to keep moving from the stave to read duration:

The traditional practice of notating tied initial note-values to indicate a moving pitch is confusing for a performer who has already moved off the note. Furthermore, the collision of noteheads and glissando line tends to make them obscure each other (a). Avoid replacing glissando durations with rests or bracketed rests as these are disconcerting (b); always use note-values for continuous sound:

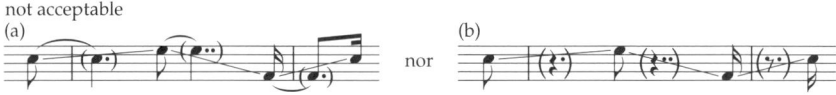

Articulation during a glissando

Use stems close to or attached to the glissando line, to indicate articulation during a glissando:

Glissando line indicating pitch contour

It is best to clarify verbally any unusual glissando notation, e.g. 'glissando to raise and lower pitch so as to reflect contour of line'.

A glissando line may be curved to any contour in order to give a better graphic description of the resultant sound than straight lines:

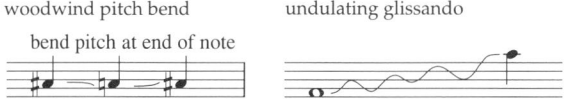

For wind players, works in the jazz medium use a diagonal trill line or curved glissando line to 'swoop onto' or 'fall off' a note, usually from or to an unspecified pitch. The most common term for sliding onto a specified note that is transferred to the classical repertoire is the 'rip'.

Vibrato

A specific intensity of vibrato (abbrev. *vib.*) may be requested, which differs from the normal vibrato used by wind and string players and singers. The specification may be for speed (*fast* or *slow vibrato*) or for amplitude (*wide vibrato*, *¼-tone vibrato*, etc.); for much vibrato (*molto vib.*) or for exaggerated vibrato (*vib. esag.*).

Senza vib./*non vib.* ('without vibrato') is an instruction to suppress normal vibrato (indicated *vib. norm.* or *ord.* after a contrary instruction). It is confusing to abbreviate either *non vib.* or *vib. norm.* to *n.v.*

A vibrato style is indicated verbally above the stave, and followed either by a dotted line for its duration (bars 1–2), or cancelled by a further instruction (last bar):

To indicate gradual changes in vibrato, place an arrow between instructions:

An unshaded wavy line (not the shaded trill line) may replace verbal instructions to indicate visually that vibrato should change. Such graphic representation is necessary only when frequent verbal indications would otherwise congest the appearance of the music. Increase and decrease of vibrato speed, width, or both (according to the given definition) are reflected by corresponding changes in the contour of the wavy line:

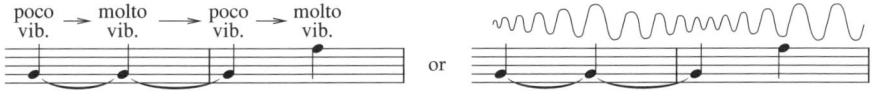

This graphic notation requires an explanatory note, e.g. 'Increase and decrease vibrato speed and width with the corresponding line depth.'

6
Metre

CONTENTS

Introduction 151

Time signatures 151

Beaming according to the metre 153

Grouping inner beams 156

Horizontal position of rests 159

Grouping rests according to the metre 160

Beaming across rests 164

Sustaining notes across beats 166

Beaming to reflect musical structure 169

Syncopation 170

Cross rhythm 171

Interchanging simple- and compound-time metres 172

Polymetre 174

Metres of variable stress 178

Mixed metres (Alternating time signatures) 179

Denominator as any division of the semibreve 180

Denominator as notehead 182

Tempo indications 182

Tempo equations 185

Pauses 187

Silent bars (G.P.) 190

Introduction

Barring for practicality

Notated metre represents a pattern of accented and unaccented beats within a bar. For some composers the implied hierarchy of accent within metre is not relevant and they use barring solely for convenience: for the practical purposes of conducting, for co-ordination in unconducted music and to facilitate reading rhythm in manageable bar lengths. Accents are notated where they are required, but otherwise the beginning and subdivisions of the bar are not intended to be stressed. Such scores should indicate that barlines are for co-ordination only and have no function as metric accentuation. Ligeti notes this in some of his scores (see, for example, the Chamber Concerto and *Ramifications*).

Barring for metrical purposes

Composers for whom the hierarchy of accent is relevant will select one time signature in preference to another to determine the placing of such implied accents. For example, $\frac{3}{4}$, $\frac{6}{8}$ and $\frac{12}{16}$ are of equal bar length (twelve semiquavers) but $\frac{3}{4}$ has three stresses, $\frac{6}{8}$ has two stresses, $\frac{12}{16}$ has four stresses:

A time signature will be associated with its specific beat stresses unless the musical content contradicts them (see *Cross rhythm*, p. 171).

Rhythms, including rests, are specifically grouped so that the eye can identify where the beats of the bar fall (see *Beaming according to the metre*, p. 153, *Grouping inner beams*, p. 156, and *Grouping rests according to the metre*, p. 160).

Time signatures

Definition

The upper figure of the time signature, the numerator, shows the number of note-values contained in the bar as expressed by the lower figure. The lower figure, the denominator, is the number of those note-values that, together, add up to a semibreve (thus $\frac{3}{4}$ = 3 crotchets in a bar, $\frac{6}{8}$ = 6 quavers in a bar). In other words, the denominator is the division of the semibreve into equal parts:

(See also *Denominator as any division of the semibreve*, p. 180.)

Size and placing

Time-signature numerals should exactly fill the height of the stave. Smaller numerals are not sufficiently conspicuous:

Time-signature numerals use a unique heavy font so that they stand out as clearly as possible against the stave. The font distinguishes them from other numerals so that the eye identifies them instantly.

Time signatures are sometimes placed above the stave in scores with a small stave size so as to be more conspicuous. In an instrumental part or playing score, the best position for a time signature is always on the stave so that the eye of the performer following his or her own line does not need to leave the stave to take in a time change.

At the beginning of a piece, the time signature goes after a clef and any key signature. It holds good for a whole movement or up to a change of metre. It should be repeated at the beginning of a new movement, even if this is the same as that of the previous movement, and even when the music follows on from the previous movement without a break.

Placing time-signature changes

The new time signature is always placed after the barline.

When a change of time signature occurs between systems, add a cautionary indication at the end of the first system, after the last barline:

A thin double barline precedes a change of time signature only when one coincides with a new musical section.

Beaming according to the metre

Divisions of a beat are beamed together in all metres, in order to simplify reading beats:

metres of 2 beats

metres of 3 beats

metres of 4 beats

In 2/4 and in 3/4, any number of quavers can be beamed together:

This is provided that groups in 3/4 do not give the appearance of 6/8 accentuation. For example, the following common figurations should be notated thus:

The second example incorrectly implies 6/8 accentuation. (Music from the Classical and Romantic periods frequently uses this beaming – the context makes it clear that cross rhythm is not intended.)

(See also *Dividing notes in three-beat and compound-time metres*, p. 168.)

In 4/8 and in 4/4, groups of semiquavers and quavers respectively may be beamed into half-bars:

However, notes should never be beamed over the middle of the bar, since the third beat carries a secondary stress which should always be indicated in the notation:

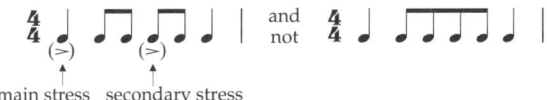

main stress   secondary stress

If in doubt – and for utmost clarity – beam together only the notes of a single beat. In the following example the quavers in 2/4 are beamed into single beats to make clear the different accentuation from the 6/8 dotted-crotchet beat:

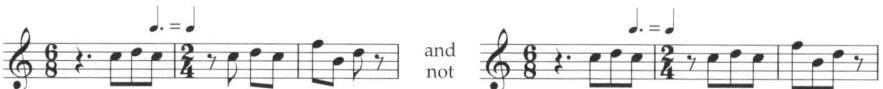

Beams joining two or three beats may also be separated to indicate a change of pitch pattern:

Beaming must not obscure bar division in any metre (see Table 1, opposite; see also *Metres of variable stress*, p. 178).

QUAVER-BEAT METRES

It is acceptable to beam together groups of two and three quavers, provided that inner beams are divided to indicate the quaver beats:

SEMIQUAVER-BEAT METRES

Groups of two or three beats may be joined together, provided that the innermost beam is divided to indicate the semiquaver beats (semiquaver beams must join semiquaver beats):

(See also *Grouping inner beams*, p. 156.)

COMPOUND TIME

Beams join notes within a beat, never across a beat. The dotted lines in Table 1 (opposite) show this.

6/4 is a compound-time metre (𝅗𝅥. + 𝅗𝅥.). It is sometimes used in alternation with crotchet metres (4/4 etc.) to mean 3/2 (𝅗𝅥 + 𝅗𝅥 + 𝅗𝅥) in order to indicate a continuing crotchet beat. Although not strictly correct, this convention is permissible – as long as the accentuation of the bar is clarified by correct 3/2 grouping of both note-values and rests.

BEAMING ACCORDING TO THE METRE

TABLE 1: Beaming according to the metre

Beams must not cross the indicated vertical dotted lines.
The boxes contain the notated duration of a whole bar for the given time signatures on that line.

Grouping inner beams

Groups of notes are clearest to read when they are subdivided into small units.

In crotchet and dotted-crotchet metres, separate inner beams into quaver units:

This is much easier to read than when the beams are undivided:

not recommended

Groups of semiquavers are not usually separated into quaver units:

except in a dotted-crotchet metre that follows on from a dissimilar beat division:

In $\frac{3}{8}$, groups of semiquavers (or shorter note-values) must be separated into quaver units since this is a three-beat metre:

SUBDIVISIONS WITHIN A QUAVER UNIT

For clarity, groups of short note-values should divide into semiquaver units:

The number of beams separating the groups is equal to the duration of the groups they separate:

GROUPING INNER BEAMS 157

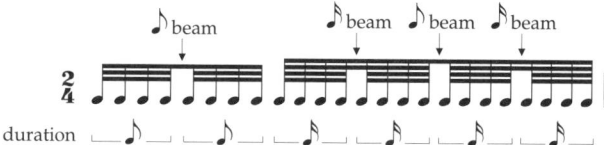

In other words, semiquaver beams must join groups that add up to the value of a semiquaver – it is incorrect for only a quaver beam to do this:

SCALE PASSAGES

It is acceptable for beams to remain undivided, to show that there should be no internal stresses (although the rhythm will be harder to read when there are, say, twelve or more notes):

(See also *Beaming to reflect musical structure*, p. 169.)

Fractional beams

A note-value that is only a fraction of a beat takes a fractional beam. This beam points in the direction of the beat or division of the beat to which it belongs:

(For fractional beam design, see p. 17.)

In ¾ and in compound-time dotted-crotchet metres (e.g. ⁶⁄₈), a fractional beam that is part of a second quaver must point in the direction of the second quaver:

Reversing the beam indicates that the semiquaver belongs to a dotted-quaver beat:

Fractional beams point away from a rest so as to stay inside the main beam. They should remain separate from their neighbouring inner beams in order to show that they are a fraction of a beat only:

It is equally acceptable to point beams towards the rests, to clarify the metrical grouping:

Alternatively, beams may be extended across rests, to occupy whole beats (see *Extending beams to cover whole beats*, p. 165).

Beamed groups indicating variation in speed

A group with fanned beams indicates free accelerando or rallentando within the duration of a group of notes.

The group uses two or three beams at its fastest point; the beams converge at the slowest point:

(a)

Such beams may extend across a barline:

(b)

If it is necessary to indicate the duration of the group, place a small note-value over the group, enclosed within a square bracket:

(c)

The notes of the group may either be spaced evenly (as in (a), above), or else spaced proportionally to their speed: i.e. the slower notes are spaced further apart than the faster ones ((b) and (c), above).

Horizontal position of rests

Position a rest exactly as if it were a note of the equivalent duration:

A rest is always placed at the start of its duration, never in the centre of a beat:

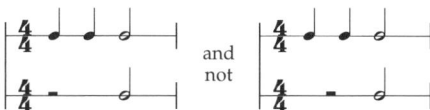

The only exception is for whole-bar rests (see below).

When another part contains grace notes, rests align with the measured note:

(For placing rests on and around the stave, see *Vertical placing of rests within the stave*, p. 35.)

Whole-bar rests

The semibreve rest is placed at the visual centre of the bar, or immediately to the left of a central duration. When the bar has evenly spaced beats, the rest will come just before the middle note-value:

Even when the middle rhythmic point is far off-centre, the whole-bar rest goes at the visual centre of the bar:

When the rest bar contains a clef, key signature or time signature, place the rest at the centre of the remaining blank space:

The semibreve rest acts as a whole-bar rest in any time signature (but see below). For all time signatures of 4/2 or 8/4 and over, the breve rest represents a whole-bar rest:

Place a semibreve rest at the beginning of its duration when it represents the sum of four crotchet rests, e.g. for a half-bar of 4/2.

ALTERNATIVE NOTATION: RESTS TAILORED TO THE METRE

The value of the actual rest in the respective time signature may be used on a one-off or occasional basis. For example, in music of rhythmically complex and constantly changing metres, this may help a performer to read at speed:

Align each rest as if it were its equivalent note-value:

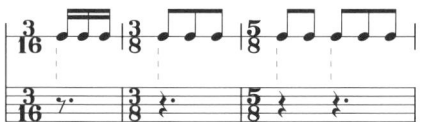

(See also *Metres of variable stress*, p. 178.)

When the metrical patterns are not complex, this notation tends to look unnecessarily fussy. The established convention of using semibreves for all rests means that they are automatically read in combination with a time signature, making rest symbols for individual bar lengths redundant.

Grouping rests according to the metre

Rests must be grouped to clarify the divisions of the bar. Rests with the duration of one or more beats may start only on a beat.

Rests in metres of two and four beats divide to expose the middle of the bar (marked by dotted lines):

simple time

compound time

The rests marked ⌐, above, may be amalgamated (see *Compound Time*, p. 163).

In metres of three beats, rests must show all beats (a two-beat rest belongs to a metre of two or four beats):

Dotted rests

Older editions do not use dotted rests:

However, beats are more compact and thus easier to read when rests within a beat are combined:

SIMPLE TIME

Rests at the beginning and end of beats: the recommended practice is to use dotted rests at the beginning but not at the end of a beat. This visually identifies on which part of the beat the rests fall:

It is acceptable to use dotted rests at both the beginning and the end of a beat, although the visual difference between the types of rest is lost:

The longest permitted dotted rest is one value smaller than the beat. In crotchet metres, the longest dotted rest is a dotted quaver:

(See also *Double-dotted rests*, below.)

In minim metres, the longest dotted rest is a dotted crotchet:

The dotted-minim rest is normally never used in simple time. The only exception is to show units of three crotchets in time signatures such as $\frac{5}{4}$ and also $\frac{7}{4}$ (see *Metres of variable stress*, p. 178).

Double-dotted rests: these may replace two or more rests within a beat:

When it is useful to differentiate rests before and after a beat, use the double dotting only at the beginning of a beat:

When it is preferable to show more clearly how the beat is divided, divide the rest into half-beats:

Rests in the middle of a beat: these should expose the middle of a beat:

$\frac{2}{4}$ ♪ 𝄾 𝄾 ♪. ♪𝄾 | or $\frac{2}{4}$ ♪𝄾 𝄾 ♪. ♪𝄾 | but not $\frac{2}{4}$ ♪𝄾 ♪. ♪𝄾 |

but may be combined when rhythms are straightforward:

$\frac{2}{4}$ ♪𝄾 ♪♪𝄾 ♪|

COMPOUND TIME

The dotted rest as a whole beat differentiates compound- from simple-time metres.

Whole beats may be combined as long as the rests do not obscure the important divisions of the bar (shown by the dotted lines in Table 1, p. 155). Otherwise, no rest should be written across a beat:

$\frac{12}{8}$ 𝄻 . | 𝄾 ♩. | ♩. 𝄾 | 𝄻 . |

Rests within a beat: rests at the beginning of a beat may be combined:

$\frac{6}{8}$ 𝄾 ♪𝄾 ♪|

When there are alternative ways of combining rests, it is better to indicate the second rather than the third division of the beat, since this clarifies the divisions more quickly:

$\frac{6}{8}$ 𝄾 𝄾. ♪𝄾 | rather than $\frac{6}{8}$ 𝄾 𝄾 𝄾 ♪𝄾. |

(This same principle applies to note divisions: see *Dividing notes in three-beat and compound-time metres*, p. 168.)

Rests that follow a beat should expose all three divisions:

$\frac{6}{8}$ ♪ 𝄾 𝄾 ♪𝄾 𝄾 𝄾 |

If it is important for a performer to sense all three divisions of an accompanying part, rests at the beginning of the beat should show these:

$\frac{6}{8}$ 𝄾 𝄾 ♪𝄾 𝄾 ♪| 𝄾 𝄾 𝄾 ♪𝄾 𝄾 𝄾 ♪|

Otherwise it is better to combine the rests, as this clarifies the position of beats, especially in long bars:

In the middle of a beat, rests must expose at least two of the three divisions. Indicate all three divisions if this is important to the musical sense:

Beaming across rests

It is helpful to beam notes across rests within the beat in order to identify the position of the beats easily. Beats containing rests are grouped in the same way as if the rests were equivalent note-values (see *Beaming according to the metre*, p. 153).

It is very useful to beam together each beat in compound time:

as this is much quicker to read than separate stems:

When there are repeated rhythmic patterns of quavers in a crotchet metre, any number of quavers may be beamed together in $\frac{2}{4}$ and $\frac{3}{4}$:

and half-bars beamed together in $\frac{4}{4}$:

Rhythmic figures that are not part of a repeated pattern may be best beamed into separate beats, so that they are not mistaken for triplets nor for groups of three quavers in compound time:

DIVIDING INNER BEAMS FOR RESTS

Inner beams may remain unbroken if equivalent note-values would have unbroken beams:

However, except for the above patterns of alternating notes and rests, inner beams look more elegant separated by the rests:

rather than

(For positioning rests with beams, see *Beams across rests*, p. 36.)

Extending beams to cover whole beats

Beams may extend across rests that start or finish a beat, in order to clarify the position of a beat. Stemlets (stems that stop short of the rest) mark the position of each rest, and inner beams are then extended or attached to these stemlets.

This notation is helpful for passages of complex rhythms, especially where rests occupy the start or finish of a subdivision of a beat, since the extended beams then identify the subdivisions:

Extended beams may replace dotted lines that might otherwise be necessary (or, at the very least, helpful) to delineate beats in long bars of short note-values. This notation is well suited to the rhythmic complexity of such composers as Elliott Carter (see, for instance, *A Symphony of Three Orchestras*).

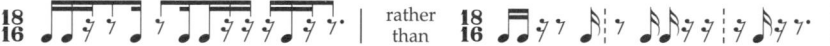

In the case of tuplets, the numeral centres above or below the beam, dispensing with the need for a bracket:

(See *When to use brackets*, p. 199.)

Use extended beams only when it is essential to help the reader to identify the beats. Elsewhere, use traditional beaming, since otherwise the extra notation makes straightforward rhythms look unnecessarily complicated:

Sustaining notes across beats

Note-values sustained across a beat or half-bar must expose the beat structure of the bar:

and not

Three-beat metres must show two out of three beats:

(See also *Dividing notes in three-beat and compound-time metres*, p. 168.)

Only very straightforward rhythms may be written across the beat or half-bar:

(See also *Syncopation*, p. 170.)

As the division of a bar becomes more complex, it is essential to reveal more of the beats:

each beat indicated

rather than

each half-beat indicated

Dividing long notes according to the metre

SIMPLE TIME

A long duration that starts on the beat may be written as a single note-value:

When the rhythms are not part of a regular pattern, the long duration may be divided to expose the beats or half-bar, to make the rhythm easier to count and therefore to place. In 4/4 it is the third (not the fourth) beat that should be exposed:

Some composers prefer to divide a long note that is followed by a rest into its separate beats, in order to emphasize that the note should be held for its full value:

A long duration that starts after the beat is usually divided to show further beats. This helps the placing of the second note:

COMPOUND TIME

No note-value should be written across the beat, except combined whole beats:

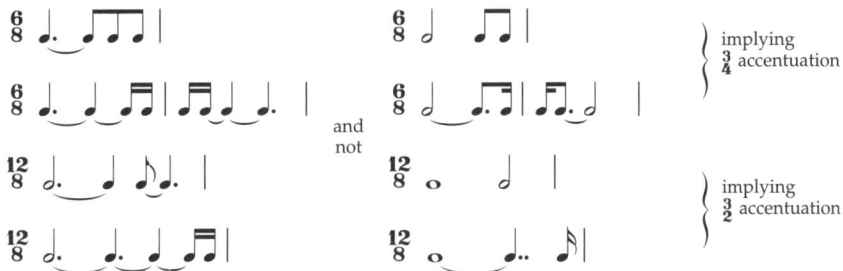

Dividing notes in three-beat and compound-time metres

Metres of three beats must expose at least two. Compound-time metres must show at least two out of three divisions of the beat. Not to do so may imply a different pattern of stresses (see column *Division into 2 beats*, below; see also *Grouping to contradict the metre*, opposite).

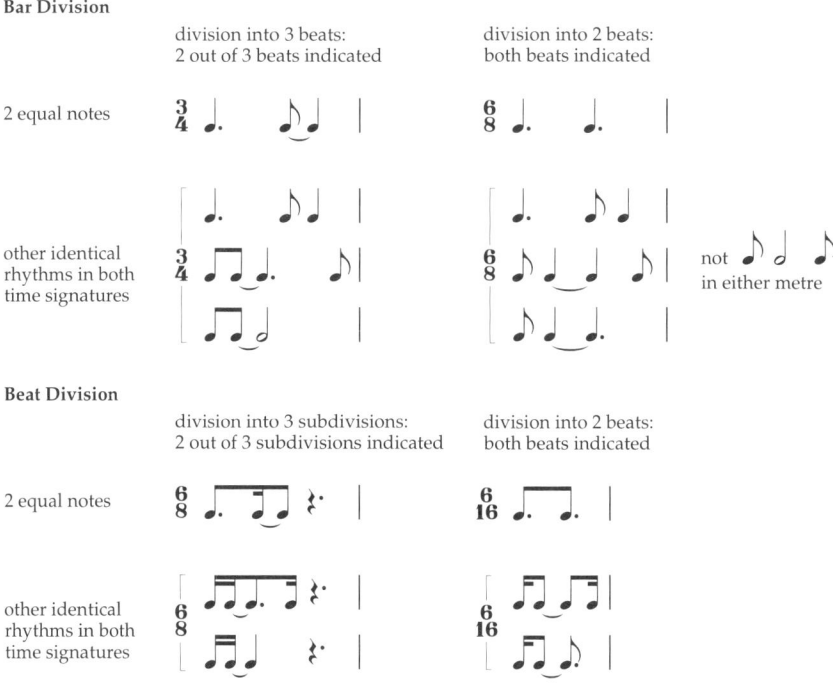

(See also *Compound-time duplet divisions*, p. 204.)

When there is the option to expose either a tied second or third beat (or division of a beat), indicate the second if this most quickly clarifies the structure of the bar:

Indicate the third beat or division when this makes the rhythm simpler to read:

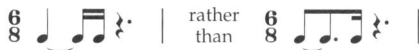

GROUPING TO CONTRADICT THE METRE

When the bar is to be stressed contrary to the metre – three-beat metres into two, two-beat metres into three – group the rhythms as if in the opposing metre:

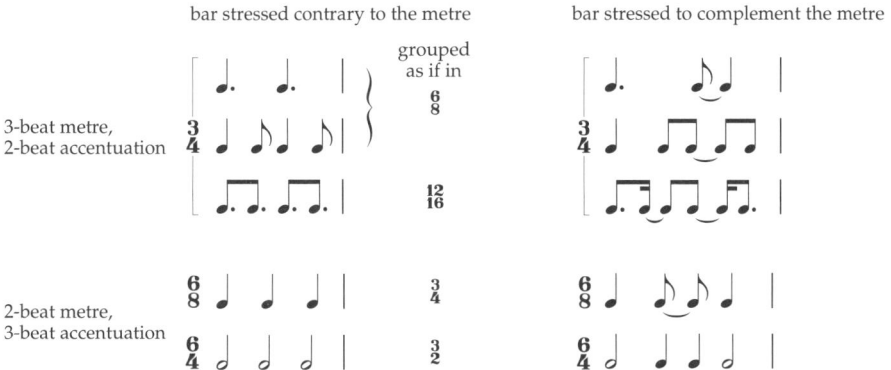

(See also *Syncopation*, p. 170.)

Beaming to reflect musical structure

The demands of fast reading are best served when articulation marks alone illustrate the musical structure, leaving the note-grouping to indicate the metre, syncopation or cross rhythm.

Composers have always arranged beaming in unconventional ways, in order to point aspects of the musical structure. They sometimes prefer not to divide beams, to discourage any accentuation of subdivisions within expressive passages (this notation is not recommended):

In a different context, a composer may divide a beam to coincide with changes in articulation and dynamics. Only when rhythms are straightforward and bars short might it be beneficial to use such notation:

Debussy: *Ibéria*

To use separate tails to convey the impression of short notes is extremely unhelpful:

and not

Syncopation

Note-values written across the metre, contradicting normal bar division, express accents superimposed on the basic metre. Note-grouping that contradicts the metre will be read as syncopation. (Examples of this are shown under *Grouping to contradict the metre*, first column, p. 169.)

When accentuation is intended to contradict the basic metre, write note-values across the beats:

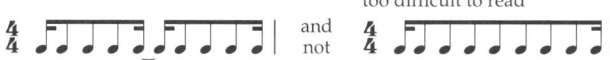

Divide up long bars of short note-values so that the reader does not lose count of the basic metre:

In a slow tempo, the syncopated rhythms may be divided into groups of tied single beats (rhythms notated as shown in first example opposite, lowest line 'within ♩ beat').

Rhythms that should not be syncopated must divide note-values to expose the beats of the bar:

The following common patterns are exceptions and should always be written as follows:

Cross rhythm

Cross rhythm is the shifting of metre across the barline as well as within the bar. It is the imposition of a different metrical grouping without reinstatement of the given metre.

Cross rhythm is used in ensemble music to notate non-coinciding rhythmic stresses. Except in chamber music, it is generally impractical to write simultaneously different bar lengths for different musicians (see *Non-coinciding bar lengths*, p. 175).

For most practical purposes, the marking of stresses counter to the metre is the most helpful notation, as it enables the performer to continue thinking in the written metre and not across it:

Schoenberg's stress symbols are used for this very purpose (see *Stress symbols introduced by Schoenberg*, p. 115).

Alternatively, square brackets above the stave may show the cross rhythm:

When note-grouping contradicts the metre in order to express the cross rhythm, square brackets or extra accentuation marks are redundant:

Changing beaming in this way should be used with great care: when the performer is forced to think across the beat it is all too easy to lose count.

(See also *A division of the beat remaining constant*, p. 172.)

Where rhythms are already complex, the rhythms of the superimposed stresses may be notated above the stave, while the rhythmic grouping on the stave conforms to the time signature:

Birtwistle: *Secret Theatre*

To show a superimposed metre in a complex passage, the cross rhythm may be placed on a line and given the time signature of its true accentuation. Barlines may not necessarily coincide with the instrumental part. The chamber music of Elliott Carter provides many instances of this notation (see, for instance, String Quartets Nos. 1–3).

Interchanging simple- and compound-time metres

It must be quite clear whether it is a division of the beat or the whole beat that remains constant.

A division of the beat remaining constant

To indicate the relationship between the two metres, state the equivalent note-values (i.e. the metric equation) over the barline at the first appearance:

Alternatively, for bars that contradict the prevailing metre, add a time signature in brackets appropriate for the accentuation. Restate the initial metre where relevant. It is unnecessary to state the note-value equation as well, as the brackets surrounding a time signature always mean that the bar has the duration of the previous metre:

INTERCHANGING SIMPLE- AND COMPOUND-TIME METRES 173

When rhythms are straightforward, it is sufficient for the note-grouping to indicate the cross rhythm without spelling out the additional metre:

The beat remaining constant

When the beat is to remain constant, simple- and compound-time metres may be interchanged in order to save writing triplets in simple time, duplets and quadruplets, and so on, in compound time. The ratio of compound- to simple-time metre is 3:2:

	compound time		simple time		ratio	
2-beat metres	**6/4** (𝅗𝅥. beat)	=	**2/2** (𝅗𝅥 beat)		3:2	𝅗𝅥
	6/8 (♩. beat)	=	**2/4** (♩ beat)		3:2	♪
3-beat metre	**9/16** (♪ beat)	=	**3/8** (♪ beat)		3:2	𝅘𝅥𝅯

Indicate the relationship between the metres as a note-value equation over the barline at the first exchange both to and from the different time signature:

(See also *Tempo equations*, p. 185.)

CONCURRENT SIMPLE- AND COMPOUND-TIME METRES

Different metres may be used simultaneously on different staves of a score or in a two-stave part. Notate the passage initially in the most prevalent metre, and change the time signature for a stave as required. Place brackets around the time-signature changes, both to and from the less prevalent time signature, to indicate that this is not common to all parts.

In a score, after a barline allow space in all parts for the addition of the alternative time signature. (The following is an example of extreme compression: it would not normally be worthwhile changing the time signature for less than several bars.)

DUAL TIME SIGNATURES (INTERCHANGEABLE METRES)

Use two time signatures for passages that interchange equivalent-beat simple- and compound-time metres either irregularly or simultaneously. Indicate both time signatures at the outset:

$$\tfrac{2}{4}\tbinom{6}{8} \quad \text{or} \quad \tfrac{2/6}{4/8} \quad \text{or} \quad \tfrac{2=6}{4\ 8}$$

Notate each bar according to the most appropriate metre. When the dual time signatures follow on from another metre, the time signature placed first is the one with the same written beat as the previous metre:

Notate whole-bar notes in the prevailing metre:

Note that the statement of interchanging metres such as $\tfrac{2}{4}\tbinom{6}{8}$ is not the same as $\tfrac{2}{4}+\tfrac{6}{8}$, which is a strict alternation of the two metres (see *Mixed metres (Alternating time signatures)*, p. 179).

Polymetre

Any number of simultaneous metres may be used for different parts. Allocate specific time signatures for individual staves as required.

Simultaneous metres must follow correct rhythmic alignment. Align equivalent beats (where these occur), and place non-equivalent beats according to their correct relationships to other note-values.

Coinciding barlines

If practical, different time signatures in different parts can simplify the notation of complex rhythmic relationships:

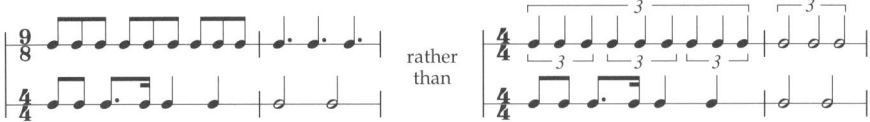

In the previous example the equivalent note-value ratio is 9:8 quavers. It is helpful to define this metrical relationship at the outset of the polymetre (place it above the top stave):

$$\frac{4}{4}\ o\ =\ \frac{9}{8}\ \text{♩. ♩.}$$

Select the closest metrical equivalent in duration, in this case 9:8 quavers – so that the note-values of the different metres are as close in duration as they can be – not, for example, 9:4 quavers:

The following concurrent time signatures occur in Vaughan Williams's Sixth Symphony. The $\frac{2}{2}$ functions as both a two-beat metre with the $\frac{6}{4}$ and a four-beat metre with the $\frac{12}{8}$:

Rhythmic breakdown of Vaughan Williams: Symphony No. 6, first movement, fig. 8

Non-coinciding bar lengths

The true metrical stress of individual parts may be expressed as independent metres, to result in non-coinciding bar lengths. This may replace the notation of cross rhythm (see *Cross rhythm*, p. 171), but is generally impractical except in chamber music.

Where possible, select metres that share a common beat or common division of the beat. Thus, in a score, the common value can be vertically aligned:

(This is also the case in Ravel's Piano Trio, second movement, figs. 10–15.)

When a note aligns with the first beat of a bar in another part, the rhythmic values should align with each other, and not with a barline.

When note-values between parts are not equivalent, it is important to define the relationships of the different parts. When the polymetre occurs at the outset, indicate the note-value equation as in the example above.

When the polymetre starts after the beginning of the piece, define metrical relationships with surrounding metres at the points of divergence and convergence. The following condensed section of score (violin parts omitted) shows the concurrent metres and how to indicate them:

Bliss: Oboe Quintet
(oboe and viola have the same metrical relationship to the bass line)

RHYTHMIC RELATIONSHIP GRID

Where the relationship between metres is complex, it may be essential to clarify how the different metres coincide. In a score, it may be helpful to provide a rhythmic grid (a cue line of rhythm) to show how the conductor's beats (or beats of the majority of the ensemble) relate to the differing metre.

Notate the conductor's (or ensemble's) beats in the opposing metre (see, for example, Adès, *Asyla*, Ecstasio, Letter L; Maxwell Davies's *Hymn to St Magnus*, Letter S ff also uses a rhythmic grid to show how the parts co-ordinate).

Likewise provide this rhythm cue in the parts of players who play in a different metre from the more prevalent one: these players need to measure their music against the prevalent metre. (Conductor beats, given as note-values for the relevant beats, would be added to the 'orchestra metre' cue line.)

Where helpful, the rhythmic grid should notate the rhythms of the other player(s) in the metre of the relevant player's part (see, for example, Adès, Piano Quintet, Fig. 11 ff.).

Parts in different tempi (Poly-tempo)

The use of simultaneous different tempi may be required to be co-ordinated (e.g. by a second conductor, a click-track, or by the players themselves) or else not precisely co-ordinated. When there are equivalent ratios between tempi, a score should rhythmically align the parts according to these ratios. In the following table the tempi have the exact ratio 4:5:6:7. The second column gives an alternative notation in a single metre, which would be the traditional way of indicating these tempo relationships:

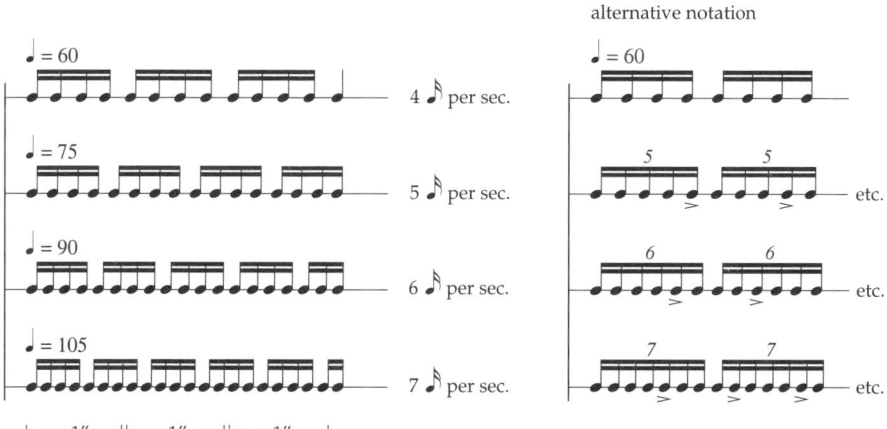

Whether or not the different tempi form precise ratios, a score should align parts as precisely as possible (see, for example, Stockhausen's *Gruppen*). Where exact co-ordination is not required, the result may not be precisely the same from one performance to the next; the score will, however, present one possible sequence of events (see, for instance, Boulez's *Rituel: in memoriam Bruno Maderna*). The layout principles are the same as when an individual part is completely independent: the independent parts should be marked as *independently* or *own tempo* to clarify that there is no fixed rhythmic alignment.

Metres of variable stress

Where possible, bar division is indicated by beam grouping:

or by the particular division of longer notes and rests:

(See also Table 1, p. 155.)

Otherwise, divide bars by adding dotted barlines. In a score place these through each instrumental section individually (as with ordinary barlines). They may be omitted through *tacet* instrumental sections. In an instrumental part (but not a score), divide rests in a rest bar to show the bar division (see next example, last bar).

In an instrumental part, dotted barlines are very helpful, especially in complex music or long bars, since the player may well mark in the divisions of the bar in any case. Use dotted barlines in rest bars only where division would otherwise be unclear:

Indicating the numerical divisions of the bar is the most economical notation in less complex music. This is especially useful when a division remains unchanged, since numerical division holds good until contradicted. Place the numerals at the beginning of the bar – they may be bracketed or not:

Adding up the beats is likely to trip a player up in rehearsal, and so should be avoided:

not recommended

It is best not to use small notes over the relevant beats – reserve notes for playing wherever possible:

avoid

Conductor beat symbols | ⊓ △ (meaning one, two and three beats) are best avoided as well. Conductors always prefer to write in their own markings in a score, and, in parts, bar division is better expressed in one of the ways shown above.

When the division of a metre remains unchanged throughout, this may be indicated at the outset:

Mixed metres (Alternating time signatures)

A fixed pattern of alternating metres may be notated where bars of different duration alternate (as opposed to interchanging compound- and simple-time – see *Interchanging simple- and compound-time metres*, p. 172). Place the two (or more) time signatures at the start, with a '+' sign between each.

It is permissible to notate each metre as a separate bar:

However, it is more common to treat the pattern of alternating time signatures as single bars and to separate each metre with a dotted barline, if necessary (as in *Metres of mixed denominators* – see p. 180).

When metres alternate irregularly, place both time signatures at the outset, with a hyphen between them, for clarity: **2**-**3**/**4 4**

This notation is useful in chamber music, to save writing in the many alternating time signatures, although in conducted music it is better to have each time signature where required. In individual parts, rest bars will require the relevant time signature – since the player will otherwise have no indication of bar length.

Metres of mixed denominators

A fixed pattern of alternating time signatures may consist of groups that require different denominators. Between the different time signatures, any single duration is taken to be equal, i.e. the smallest unit (the semiquaver in the example below) is the same duration for all the time signatures indicated.

Each section of the bar must conform to its appropriate time signature so as to clarify the bar division. Dotted barlines may separate the different portions of the bar where this is helpful (bar 3–4):

Time signatures with numerators as fractions

Time signatures with numerators as fractions (i.e. a fraction of a beat) are an unnecessarily obscure notation. Instead, notate half-, quarter- and eighth-beats as metres of mixed denominators:

$$\tfrac{2}{4}+\tfrac{1}{8} \quad (\text{♩} \quad \text{♪}) \quad \text{and not} \quad \tfrac{2\tfrac{1}{2}}{4}$$

$$\tfrac{3}{4}+\tfrac{3}{16} \quad (\text{♩.} \quad \text{♪.}) \quad \text{and not} \quad \tfrac{3\tfrac{3}{4}}{4}$$

$$\tfrac{4}{4}+\tfrac{1}{32} \quad (\text{o} \quad \text{♪}) \quad \text{and not} \quad \tfrac{4\tfrac{1}{8}}{4}$$

All other fractions may be notated with a denominator that is a division of the semibreve.

Denominator as any division of the semibreve

Since the denominator is the division of the semibreve into equal parts, it may represent any number of equal divisions of the semibreve, not just the traditional multiples of two. For example, in $\tfrac{4}{6}$, the semibreve is divided into six parts to provide a note-value (triplet crotchets) of which there are four:

Thus this notation may define differing bar lengths that would otherwise require a tempo equation for every time signature change:

TABLE 2: Denominators

denominator	note-value in the time of a semibreve	examples of note-values of equal duration (but different bar lengths)
2	♩ ♩	
3	𝅗𝅥 𝅗𝅥 𝅗𝅥 (3)	4/2 ... 4/3 ...
4	♩ ♩ ♩ ♩	
5	♩ ♩ ♩ ♩ ♩ (5)	4/4 ... 2/5 ...
6	♩ ♩ ♩ ♩ ♩ ♩ (6)	2/4 ... 2/6 ...
7	♩ ♩ ♩ ♩ ♩ ♩ ♩ (7)	
8	♫ ♫ ♫ ♫	
9	♫ ♫ ♫ ♫ ♫ (9)	4/4 ... (9:8) 2/9 ...
10	♫ ♫ ♫ ♫ ♫ (5) (5)	
11	♫ ♫ ♫ ♫ ♫ ♫ (11)	
12	♫ ♫ ♫ ♫ ♫ ♫ (6) (6)	2/4 ... (3)(3) 5/12 ...

The decision as to whether to use these unconventional time signatures will depend on context. Where they are unfamiliar and are required only for a few bars, introducing them may cause unnecessary difficulty.

For performers unlikely to be familiar with the notation, provide an explanatory note such as '5/10 = a bar of five beats, each of which is 1/10 of a semibreve'.

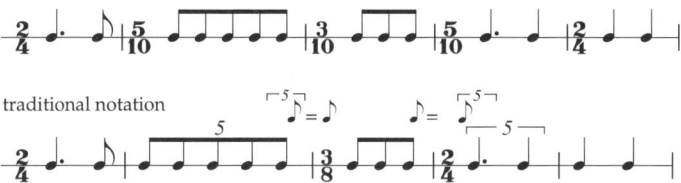

Denominator as notehead

To substitute a note-value for a denominator numeral is usually best avoided so as not to confuse the time signature with a note-value to be sounded:

A notehead used for an unconventional denominator:

is written equally efficiently as the conventional **15/16** with (**2+3** sempre) indicated above the first bar.

Tempo indications

Design

Tempo indications are printed in bold roman type and are usually larger than other text so as to be very conspicuous. The only exception is when a *rubato* marking such as *accel.* or *rall.* refers to a single line (e.g. a soloistic passage in an ensemble piece) and is not a general tempo change for the whole ensemble. Such an indication uses small italic type, as an expression mark would.

Older scores use small italic type for general indication of gradual tempo change (*accel.*, *rall.*, etc.), but italic should be reserved for expression marks, and not used in this context.

New (established) tempi have initial capitals; temporary indications (*allargando*, *accel.*, *rall.*, etc.) do not.

Placing

Place all tempo indications above the uppermost stave, and above all other performance instructions. They should be well clear of slurs, octave signs and articulation. In orchestral and ensemble full scores, tempi are usually repeated lower down the score – typically, above a string section.

When a tempo marking coincides with a time signature indication, align the tempo with the left edge of the time signature:

When there is no new time signature, align the tempo marking with the first element of the notation (e.g. a note or accidental) after the clef and key signature. Note that when the tempo change is at the start of the bar, the marking is not placed on the barline:

Tempo indications mid-bar also align with the first notational element of the respective beat:

When a repeat sign acts as a barline, the tempo aligns with the following first element of the notation. When the repeat sign is not acting as a barline, the tempo aligns with it:

repeat sign used as barline   repeat sign at beginning of system

METRONOME MARKINGS

A metronome marking may be given alone as a tempo indication. Otherwise it follows the tempo indication. It requires brackets only to confirm a current or previously stated tempo, e.g. **Tempo I** (♩ = 56), or to clarify a tempo equation, e.g.:

$$\leftarrow ♪. = ♩ \rightarrow (♩ = 100)$$

(See also *Tempo equations*, p. 185.)

Tempo Primo and Tempo Secondo

A return to an opening tempo is marked *Tempo Primo* (abbrev. *Tempo 1°* / *Tempo I*). A return to a second tempo is marked *Tempo Secondo* (abbrev. *Tempo 2ⁿᵈᵒ* / *Tempo II*). (These tempo markings would be in bold type.)

Confirm each tempo in brackets, at least the first time the terms are used, especially when there have been intervening tempi: it must be clear which tempo is being referred to. For example, **Tempo II (Vivace** (♩ = 96)**)**.

Tempo alteration markings

HORIZONTAL ALIGNMENT

It is standard practice to place each marking a small distance above all other information on the uppermost stave. It is helpful if two or more markings on the same system can be aligned, as they can be clearly seen to relate to one another. However, it is more important that each marking is more or less a consistent height above the notation, remaining close to the music, so that tempi do not become isolated from their content, and so that they are not overlooked.

A fluctuating tempo instruction may be clarified with horizontal dashes up to a new tempo. Such lines should remain horizontal and not be angled:

and not

GRAPHICALLY NOTATED GRADUAL TEMPO CHANGE

A slanted arrow is sometimes used to emphasize or replace changing tempo indications:

However, there is little need for this extra notation when a perfectly clear method already exists. Conductors and performers prefer to mark such indications in their own ways.

INDICATING CONTINUING TEMPO CHANGE

To alert the reader to a continuing tempo alteration, repeat the marking in brackets at the start of each system, e.g. (*accel. sempre*). In addition, or instead, use horizontal dashes to the new tempo marking.

TERMINATING TEMPO CHANGE BEFORE THE NEXT TEMPO

When a new tempo marking is not a consequence of the tempo alteration, place a vertical notch at the end of the dashes:

♩ = 60   **accel.** _ _ _ **a tempo** (♩ = 60)

Instead, or as well, indicate with *subito* that the new tempo is significantly different:

♪ = 126   **poco accel.** _ _ _ _ ♪ = 192 **subito**

Tempo equations

Tempo equations indicate where there is a direct relationship between note-values at a tempo change.

Cue-sized notes above the stave indicate note-value equivalents between tempi. They must be carefully placed so as not to be ambiguous.

Traditionally before about the 1950s, a note-value equation appeared after the barline of the new tempo. For example, ♩=♩ or, more explicitly ♩=♩ **precedente** ('preceding'), meant that the new note-value (♩) was equal to the former note-value (♩).

It is best not to use this arrangement now, since contemporary practice reverses the equation (following the 'metric modulation' notation invented by Elliott Carter). The traditional equation has become ambiguous as to which note-value refers to which tempo.

Instead, centre the '=' sign of the equation over the barline, so that each note-value is clearly related to the tempo of the bar above which it is placed:

Although not strictly necessary, the addition of arrows clarifies the equation and more conspicuously separates the equation from the musical text:

When it is necessary to move the equation after the barline (e.g. at the beginning of a system or after a tempo change instruction), the arrows confirm which note-value belongs to which tempo:

Identical equivalent durations are also expressed as an equation: ♪=♪, or else with a single note-value over the barline with an arrow in the direction of each tempo: ←♪→

OVER A SYSTEM BREAK

An equation is best placed before the end of the first system, i.e. in advance of the tempo change. Confirmation of the new tempo on the new system may be helpful:

Where more convenient, the equation may be placed on the new system:

or else it may be divided between the systems: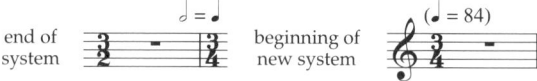

Complex metric equations

Complex ratios may require tied note-values or tuplet indications:

When the relationship between the tempi can only be expressed as a ratio: e.g. 5♪=7♪, place a tuplet indication over the cue-sized notehead (tuplet brackets may be closed – see previous example – or open-ended, as below):

$$\overset{-5\urcorner}{\leftarrow \eighthnote} = \overset{\ulcorner 7-}{\eighthnote \rightarrow} \quad \text{or} \quad \overset{5}{\leftarrow \eighthnote} = \overset{7}{\eighthnote \rightarrow}$$

For clarity, confirm these complex equations by placing a new metronome marking after the equation.

Pauses

Break in sound

The comma (') or diagonal-stroked caesura ⫽ indicates that a note is sustained for its full value, then extra time allotted for a short break in sound. The comma rather than the caesura is now more commonly used. (The caesura is also used to show damping.)

The comma usually indicates a very short break. The caesura may indicate a slightly longer break (but shorter than a pause), usually at the end of a section. For a break at the end of a bar, a pause over the barline fulfils the same function as a caesura. Both the comma and caesura may be extended with pauses (as shown under *Pause duration*, below).

Place the comma and caesura just before a subsequent note or barline. The diagonal strokes of the caesura may be up to half a beam width in thickness. The strokes are placed on the second stave-line down, extending upwards to the position of a first ledger line above the stave. In a score, the comma, caesura and pause over a barline should appear at the top of each instrumental section only (so as not to be intersected by a barline). When not over a barline, place the symbols above every stave.

Pause duration

Pauses add duration of non-specific value to the symbol above which they are placed. They may be indicated in the following ways:

short pause ⌢	*breve* ⌢	or	*poco* ⌢
long pause ⌢	*lunga* ⌢		
break with pause ⌢̓		or	⌢⫽

Pauses of different relative duration may be defined with different symbols. These must be qualified, as they do not have standard definitions. For example:

short pause ∧

long pause ⌐·⌐ ⌐·⌐|

A pause duration may be indicated in seconds over the sign:

c.5"   very long (8-10")

An indication of *a tempo* is required after a pause only when a tempo change has preceded it.

The indication *tenuto* (abbrev. *ten.*) indicates that a note should be held for its full written value. This usually implies a degree of emphasis, sometimes resulting in a brief pause. It requires no subsequent tempo clarification or *a tempo* marking.

Design and placing

The standard arc-shaped pause sign (Italian: *fermata*) is about one stave-space high, and two spaces wide (about the width of a ledger line).

The arc of the pause centres on the notehead (regardless of stem direction), rest or barline. When there are unison or adjacent notes, the pause centres on the note that is on the 'correct' side of the stem:

Always place the pause above the stave, except in double-stemmed writing (see below). It centres outside the tremolo beams of a two-note tremolo:

Place the pause further from the stave than other markings stacked on the notehead, except for the octave sign:

Mid-phrase, a pause is positioned inside a slur (as in the second two-note tremolo example opposite).

A pause must be positioned directly over a note, tremolo beam (as above), rest, barline, or sign indicating a break in sound such as a comma or caesura. Any other placing is ambiguous:

DOUBLE-STEMMED WRITING

Each separately stemmed part on a stave takes a pause. A lower part takes an inverted pause:

BRACED PART ON TWO STAVES

Although, traditionally, a single pause is often placed below a note on the lower stave regardless of its stem direction, it is more usual to place the pause above the stave.

CHORAL WRITING WITH TWO VOICES ON A STAVE

Pauses may be indicated only for the outer voices, should the pause signs for the inner voices otherwise conflict with a single, centred text:

PAUSES IN SCORE AND PARTS

The beat or subdivision on which the pause falls must agree in all parts of a score (see example under *Double-stemmed writing*, p. 189).

Since a player has only his or her own part, a long note or rest in a leading (or 'busy') part may be subdivided to indicate the precise beat or subdivision on which the pause falls. (The player would otherwise need to refer to a score.) Accompanying parts may not require this precise information, since the players will hold a pause on an existing note-value until the conductor or leader cues them.

Score and parts should agree as to whether notes or rests are subdivided to show the exact placing of the pause. Thus the conductor can see from the score the information that each part has.

Cadenzas and free passages often take pauses in accompanying or *tacet* parts.

Silent bars (G.P.)

'G.P.' ('General Pause') is used in ensemble music to indicate silence of a bar (or more) for the whole ensemble. One silent bar measured in strict time is marked *G.P.*:

This is occasionally indicated (in the same place in the bar) as *vuota* ('empty').

Multiple rests, which usually appear only as an amalgamated succession of single-bar rests in an instrumental part, may represent two or more silent bars in a score or part:

A silent bar with a pause takes a pause sign as well as a *G.P.* indication:

7
Tuplets

CONTENTS

Definition 193

The tuplet numeral 193

The tuplet bracket 194

Placing tuplet indications 197

Rhythmic alignment 200

Note-value of the tuplet 203

Stating the tuplet ratio in full 207

Degree of note division within tuplets 210

Rests within a tuplet 211

Tuplet beaming 211

Tuplets within tuplets 213

Tuplet repetition 215

Definition

A tuplet is rhythmic division that does not divide into standard groups of two or three. Such groups are considered to be 'irregular' to the regular two (♩ beat, etc.) or three (♩. beat, etc.) division. Their notation relies on adding numerals to show their different division. The difference is conceived as a distortion of the standard values. (Henry Cowell, in his *New Musical Resources*, created an imaginative alternative notation by using different-shaped noteheads for each division of the beat, although he did not apply his theory within many of his works.)

The tuplet numeral

Design and placing

The tuplet numeral is printed in italic to differentiate it from numbers referring to fingering or players, both of which are given in roman type. The height of the numeral is 1½ stave-spaces.

Place the numeral at the visual centre of the group. Thus, where the tuplet is evenly spaced, an odd-numbered numeral centres on the middle duration:

An even-numbered numeral centres between the two middle durations:

When the middle note of a tuplet subdivides, the numeral centres between an even number of subdivisions (a) and on the middle duration of an odd number of subdivisions (b):

When one part of a beat is disproportionately long visually, traditionally the numeral remains at the visual centre of the group. However, where there are complex groups of tuplets, it is more helpful if the numeral moves to the rhythmic centre of the group, even if this is visually off-centre:

(See also *Tuplets ending with the longest duration*, p. 195.)

For legibility, place numerals wholly or partially outside the stave. Those placed completely within the stave are difficult to read against the stave-lines:

The tuplet bracket

Design

The numeral should be encompassed by a square bracket, and not the curved arc of older editions, as this looks like a slur:

The bracket is broken for the numeral on which it centres vertically:

An unbroken bracket may be used and the numeral placed inside the bracket, but this arrangement takes up more vertical space than necessary:

Length of brackets

A bracket should extend from the left-hand edge of the first notehead or rest, to the right-hand edge of the final notehead or rest. It does not encompass accidentals, grace notes or an arpeggio line that precede the first note. When a final note is up-stemmed and has a tail (end of bar 2), the bracket still finishes with the stem (i.e. the right-hand edge of the note), not with the tail:

In some editions brackets finish just after the tail: this saves vertical space, as the end notch can be lowered after the stem.

TUPLETS ENDING WITH THE LONGEST DURATION

Traditionally, the bracket extends only as far as the last written duration:

Thus a numeral centred in a bracket occurs before the central duration, making the rhythm unnecessarily difficult to read. It is now usual to extend the bracket to the position of the hypothetical final division of the tuplet, so that the numeral occurs at the rhythmic centre of the group. This makes complex rhythms quicker to read:

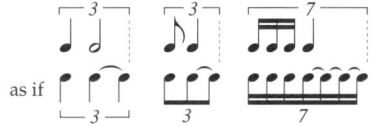

When the whole tuplet is beamed, either place the numeral in the middle of the beam:

or enclose the tuplet in a bracket that extends as far as the final (invisible) tuplet division. This allows the numeral to be at the rhythmic centre of the group:

However, such groups often occupy so small a place that there is, in practice, no room to extend a bracket.

Aligning brackets between parts

Bracket ends should align between tuplets of the same division:

When the final division of a tuplet is subdivided in some parts but not in others, the bracket ends need to extend only as far as the last duration in each group. This means that brackets may finish at different points. If preferred, all brackets may be extended to the position of the longest bracket. There is a visual logic to this, especially as uniform bracket length will allow the centred tuplet numerals to align vertically:

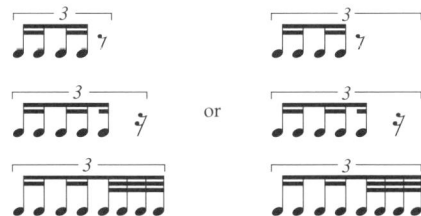

When dissimilar tuplets are present, the bracket lengths will also vary:

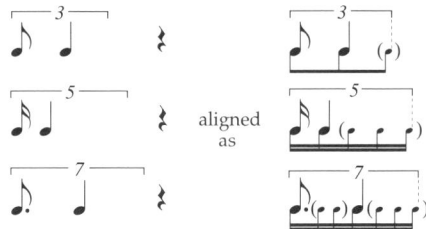

(For tuplet alignment, see Table 1, p. 201.)

Angle of brackets

GROUPS WITHOUT BEAMS

Brackets may slant in the direction of the tuplet's outer pitches:

The angle of the slant should not be too acute; match an equivalent beam slant:

Alternatively, brackets may remain horizontal. For a line of undulating groups this avoids the visual distraction of many sloping brackets:

BEAMED GROUPS

When a bracket encloses beamed notes, it should be parallel to the beams:

When the beams within a tuplet are in different directions, the bracket should remain horizontal:

The bracket should also remain horizontal where it would otherwise slope into the stave, causing a collision of lines that would obscure it:

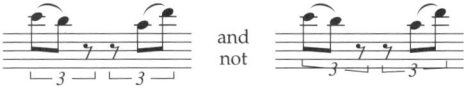

(To place tuplet indications for groups across two staves in keyboard writing, see *Placing tuplet indications*, p. 319.)

Placing tuplet indications

ABOVE OR BELOW THE STAVE

A tuplet indication normally goes to the stem side of the notes, since this is where one would expect to read the rhythm. This keeps the space on the notehead side clear for articulation and slurs:

However, in performance material with a passage requiring many ledger lines, tuplet indication may be best placed on the notehead side, as the distance between the notehead and the end of the stem is so great:

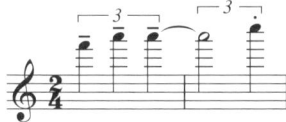

For groups with mixed stem direction, the indication can go on either side of the note. It is often best placed above the stave, as the most important consideration is that it is clear of slurs, articulation and hairpins:

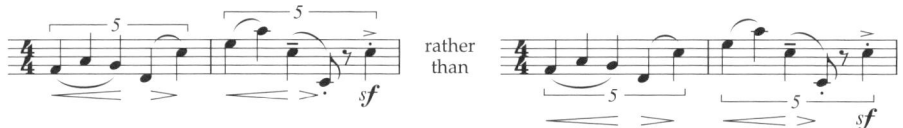

In a different context, however, indications may be best placed with the majority of stems.

If it is distracting that brackets continually alternate above and below the stave, place all brackets above the stave. The reader then becomes accustomed to seeing tuplets in one place, which helps fast reading:

BRACKETS AND SLURS

When a bracket is longer than a slur, it goes outside the slur (as in the example above). When a bracket is shorter than a slur, it goes inside it:

Place the bracket outside a slur if the two would otherwise intersect:

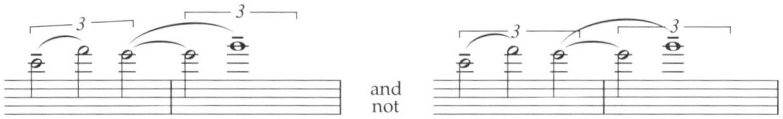

DOUBLE-STEMMED WRITING

Place brackets and numerals at the stem end of both parts. They should be further from the stave than articulation marks and also from slurs that are shorter than the brackets:

PROXIMITY TO THE STAVE

Always place the bracket outside the stave. The bracket ends and the edge of a numeral may intersect a stave-line:

When to use brackets

Use brackets to enclose partially beamed groups and groups without beams:

The bracket must enclose all the values of the tuplet, including rests:

A tuplet numeral placed on the notehead side of a group should be enclosed in a bracket to make it conspicuous:

When the whole tuplet is beamed, it is not necessary to have a bracket, provided the numeral is next to the beam:

The same is true when beams extend to enclose complete beats that include rests at either or both ends:

(See also *Extending beams to cover whole beats*, p. 165.)

A bracket must be used where a tuplet is only part of a complete beam, since the numeral might otherwise appear to apply to the entire beam:

Conversely, if there is likely to be ambiguity, a bracket should clarify that all the durations joined by a beam are part of the tuplet:

Rhythmic alignment

Tuplets must align rhythmically with all other parts (see Table 1, opposite). As with alignment in a score containing a variety of subdivided beats, this may well disrupt even spacing in another part. In the example below, the upper stave's rhythm is evenly spaced at the expense of the lower stave's rhythm. This helps reading the more complex part:

RHYTHMIC ALIGNMENT 201

TABLE 1: Alignment between ratios

How to calculate alignment

Either multiply the two ratio figures, or use the lowest common multiple. The resulting figure is the number of units to plot on a horizontal axis. Calculate the spacing of the tuplet by dividing the number of units by the tuplet:

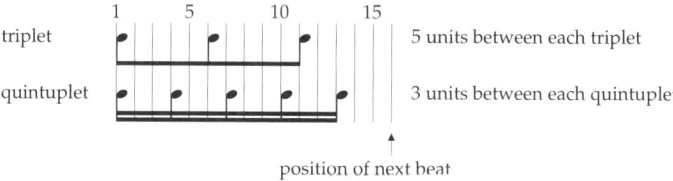

The number of units (15) ÷ the quintuplet = 3.

Place each quintuplet every three units.

triplet — 5 units between each triplet
quintuplet — 3 units between each quintuplet

position of next beat

GROUPS OF MIXED NOTE-VALUES

Identify the shortest duration of the first tuplet (x):

smallest value = ♪, and the number of small values in the unit = 10.

(If one of the groups is not a tuplet, identify the shortest duration of the beat.)

Identify the shortest duration of the second tuplet (y):

smallest value = ♪, and the number of small values in the unit = 6.

Find the lowest common multiple (LCM) of (x) and (y):

LCM (10,6) = 30

Use this number of units to plot the ratio:

30 ÷ 10 = 3 ∴ ♪ (of quintuplet) = every 3 units

30 ÷ 6 = 5 ∴ ♪ (of triplet) = every 5 units

smallest values of quintuplet
actual rhythm
smallest values of triplet
actual rhythm

Note-value of the tuplet

Principles

There are two ways to notate note-values that do not divide according to standard beat division.

Option 1 is to add extra notes to the beat until the next standard division. This can be expressed as a contracting ratio: keep the number on the left side of the ratio larger than the number on the right (see 'tuplet ratio' column). Where the left-hand number doubles the right-hand number, add another beam instead:

TABLE 2: Standard tuplet division for a crotchet

crotchet division		tuplet ratio
2	♩ ♩	
3	♩ ♩ ♩ (3)	3:2 ♪
4	♪ ♪ ♪ ♪	
5	♪ ♪ ♪ ♪ ♪ (5)	5:4 ♪
6	♪ ♪ ♪ ♪ ♪ ♪ (6)	6:4 ♪
7	♪ ♪ ♪ ♪ ♪ ♪ ♪ (7)	7:4 ♪
8	♪ ♪ ♪ ♪ ♪ ♪ ♪ ♪	
9	♪ ♪ ♪ ♪ ♪ ♪ ♪ ♪ ♪ (9)	*9:8 ♪
10	♪ ♪ ♪ ♪ ♪ ♪ ♪ ♪ ♪ ♪ (10)	10:8 ♪ up to 15:8 ♪
16	♬♬♬♬♬♬♬♬	
17	♬♬♬♬♬♬♬♬♬ (17)	17:16 ♪ up to 31:16 ♪
32	♪	

* NB: 9:8 is usually three groups of triplets: ♪♪♪ ♪♪♪ ♪♪♪ (3, 3, 3, 3)

In Option 2, the note-values take the nearest arithmetical unit, so that sevens are regarded as closer to eights than to fours. This produces a series of ratios that both contract and expand:

Option 2 makes it hard to calculate at a glance whether, for example, thirteen is closer to eight or to sixteen. In addition, triplet divisions are closer neither to the greater nor to the lesser binary values:

Option 1 – to maintain a convention where all the ratios go the same way – is recommended as the clearest notation. This avoids the contradiction of both expanding and contracting ratios.

Should tuplets be notated using expanding ratios, indicate ratios in full to avoid any confusion (see *Stating the tuplet ratio in full*, p. 207).

Compound-time duplet divisions

TRADITIONAL NOTATION

Traditional practice gives duplets and quadruplets their shorter equivalent durations even though this contradicts the contracting ratio method outlined above. 2:3 is the expanding ratio. The logic for this practice is, firstly, that the numeral acts as a substitute for a duration dot:

Secondly, when the beat remains the same, equivalent durations have identical notation in both simple- and compound-time metres. For example, where the metric equation is 2/4 ♩ = 6/8 ♩. the result is:

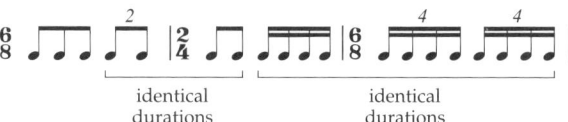

It is quite acceptable to use this traditional notation in a context where there are no tuplets more complicated than duplets or quadruplets. Where other ratios are required as well, use the contemporary notation for all ratios as described opposite.

Another convention sometimes used is to add duration dots to duplets and quadruplets while retaining the numerals. This is incorrect – the numerals are self-sufficient:

(See also *Dotted values*, below.)

CONTEMPORARY NOTATION

There are two equally valid ways of notating duplet division.

Contracting ratio: notes can be added to the beat until the next standard subdivision is reached. 4:3♪ is the contracting ratio:

(If this method is used, all other tuplet durations should also take a contracting ratio: 5:3, 7:6 etc. – see Table 3, first column, p. 206.)

Dotted values: duplet-beat divisions can take equivalent durations as dotted notes (or rests) and do not need to be written as tuplets:

♩. beat

𝅘𝅥𝅭 𝅘𝅥𝅭   𝅘𝅥𝅭 𝅘𝅥𝅭 𝅘𝅥𝅭 𝅘𝅥𝅭   𝅘𝅥𝅭 𝅘𝅥𝅭 𝅘𝅥𝅭 𝅘𝅥𝅭 𝅘𝅥𝅭 𝅘𝅥𝅭

Other tuplets may also relate to the dotted-note division:

♩. beat

⁵𝅘𝅥𝅭𝅘𝅥𝅭𝅘𝅥𝅭𝅘𝅥𝅭𝅘𝅥𝅭 = 5:4♪.   ⁷𝅘𝅥𝅭𝅘𝅥𝅭𝅘𝅥𝅭𝅘𝅥𝅭𝅘𝅥𝅭𝅘𝅥𝅭𝅘𝅥𝅭 = 7:4♪.   ¹⁰𝅘𝅥𝅭𝅘𝅥𝅭𝅘𝅥𝅭𝅘𝅥𝅭𝅘𝅥𝅭𝅘𝅥𝅭𝅘𝅥𝅭𝅘𝅥𝅭𝅘𝅥𝅭𝅘𝅥𝅭 = 10:8♪.

When using this notation, indicate the tuplet ratio and its dotted note-value at first appearance, e.g. ⌐5:4♪¬ , since the sum of the ratio note-values 4 × ♪. = ♩., 8 × ♪. = ♩. etc. is not an obvious division of a compound beat (see also Table 3, 'alternative notation' column, p. 206).

If these dotted divisions are used, all tuplets should consistently take this notation, since otherwise shorter note-values (the quintuplets below) look slower than longer values (see last example):

TABLE 3: Tuplet note-values in compound time

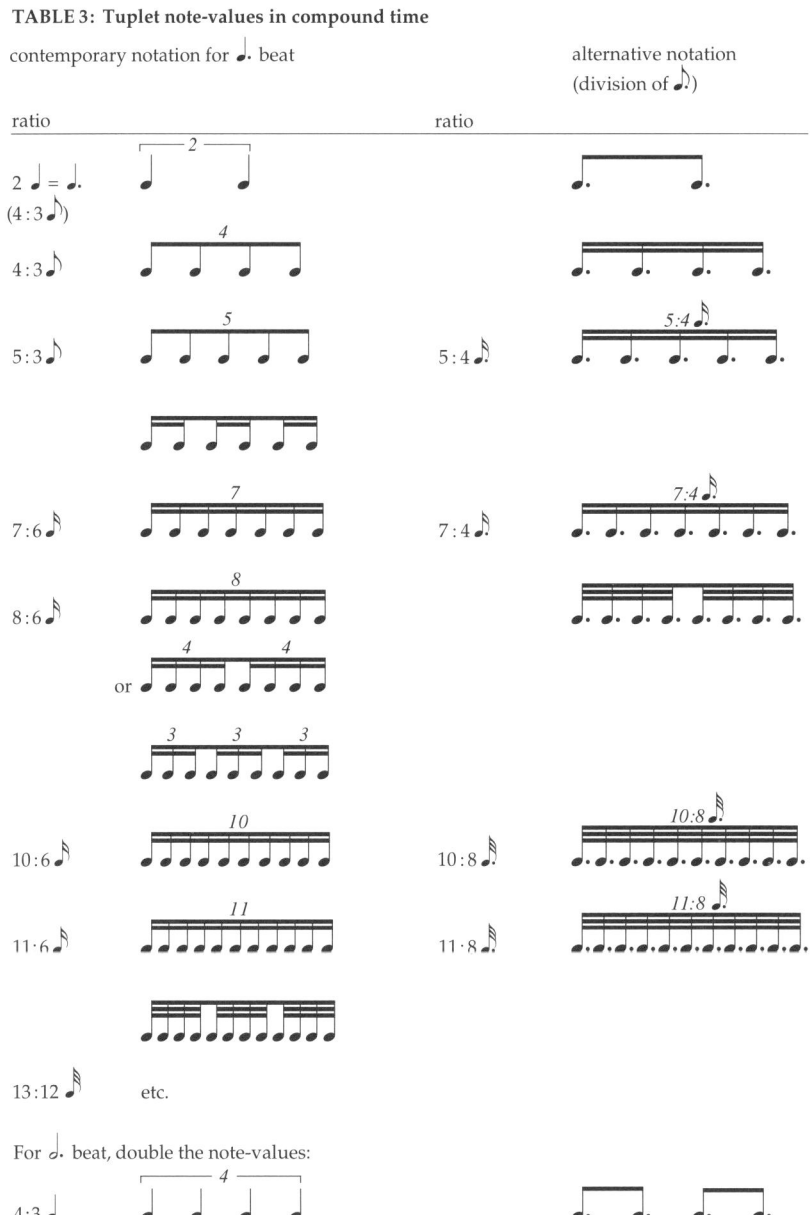

(For use of the alternative notation above, see Carter: *A Symphony of Three Orchestras*.)

Context: it is quite acceptable to use either contracting ratios or dotted notes according to whichever is most appropriate to the context:

[musical example in 9/8 with duplet, quadruplet, and octuplet groupings, or equivalent with dotted notes]

Numerals are easier to read than dotted notes except for the occasional group. The dotted divisions produce a more complicated visual image, and the reader is likely to stumble at the sudden arrival of lots of dots.

When there are extensive passages of duplets, it may be simpler to change time signature to reflect the different beat divisions (see *Interchanging simple- and compound-time metres*, p. 172).

Stating the tuplet ratio in full

State the full ratio where the tuplet is a non-standard length:

[musical example: 2/4 with 5:3 tuplet]

(The figure '5' alone would normally be 5:4 in a crotchet beat.)

In compound time, this also avoids ambiguity: for example, as to whether ⌐5¬ = 5:3 or 5:6.

The ratio should also be stated when the tuplet rhythm contains mixed note-values, and the note-value of the division is not immediately obvious:

[musical examples showing 7:4 tuplets]

When a whole bar is divided into equal tuplet values it is usually unnecessary to use a full ratio (see Table 4, p. 209).

(See also *Labelling a tuplet of mixed note-values*, p. 213.)

How to notate the ratio

Notate the ratio using a colon for 'in the time of'. Where possible, express both sides of the ratio in terms of the same note-value:

[musical examples: 2/4 with 5:4 ratio, i.e. 5♪:4♪ and not 2/4 with 5:2, i.e. 5♪:2♩]

Where the ratio cannot be expressed with the same note-value, substitute written note-values for the duration of the tuplet (see *Groups with no literal ratio equivalents*, below).

Do not notate the duration of a tuplet as an initial extra note-value, as this looks like another musical part:

Groups with no literal ratio equivalents

Where the duration of the tuplet is itself irregular – e.g. ♩♪ or a whole bar of, say, ⅝ or ⅞ – there is no straightforward unit of division against which to measure the irregularity. Notate the tuplet so as to convey an impression of equal division within the allotted duration, even though it has no literal ratio equivalent.

For division within durations of five and seven beats, select the note-value for the tuplet according to the contracting-ratio principle:

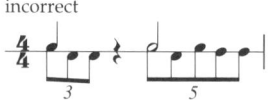

(See Table 4, opposite.)

For equal division of more unusual durations, indicate note-values on the right-hand side of the ratio to define the tuplet duration:

For rhythms indicated in Table 4, when a tempo is very slow or ensemble is critical, it may be more helpful to subdivide the bar so as to expose its beats (see 'actual rhythm' column) rather than to use contracting ratios (see *Degree of note division within tuplets*, p. 210):

STATING THE TUPLET RATIO IN FULL 209

TABLE 4: Groups with no literal ratio equivalents

	actual rhythm	written as	contracting ratios	ratio
duplet	5/8		2 (two half notes)	8:5 ♪
		or	2 (two dotted quarters)	6:5 ♪
quadruplet	5/8		4 (four quarters)	8:5 ♪
		or	4 (four dotted quarters)	6:5 ♪
triplet	5/8		3 (three quarters)	6:5 ♪
duplet	7/8		2 (two half notes)	8:7 ♪
	or 7/8			
	or* 7/8			
quadruplet	7/8		4 (four quarters)	8:7 ♪
	or* 7/8			
triplet	7/8		3 (three dotted quarters)	9:7 ♪
duplet	9/8		2 (two dotted halves)	4:3 ♩.
quadruplet	9/8		4 (four dotted quarters)	4:3 ♩.

* These undivided single durations are difficult to count in a slow tempo and are better divided up.

Degree of note division within tuplets

Tuplets may be subdivided to expose the beats of a bar when this would be helpful for ensemble purposes. The degree of note division depends on two things: the tempo, and how critical it is that the performer accurately places each note against a beat.

Undivided tuplets disregard the stresses of the written metre, in order to emphasize a fluent musical line:

Tuplets that expose the middle beat help the placing of rhythms against the middle of the bar:

When the performer needs to count each beat, expose each beat. Since performers will mark in the position of the beats that they need to 'think', it is helpful if the notation provides this:

The composer's perceived disadvantage of this notation is that it may encourage slight jerkiness or unwitting accentuation as the performer places each rhythm against the beat. To counteract this tendency, add a term such as *legato* and *scorrevole* ('flowing').

ACROSS A BARLINE

An unbroken tuplet bracket or beam may be extended between two bars. The first note-value in the second bar comes after the beginning of the bar, aligned as if the tuplet were subdivided across the barline:

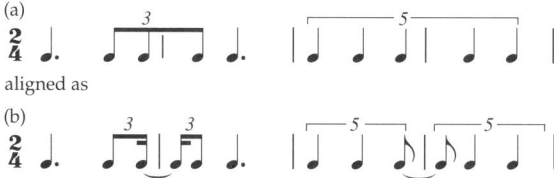

When it is more helpful to do so, subdivide tuplets to expose the beginning of each bar, as in (b) above.

When the tuplet is undivided across the barline, the number of notes on each side must be correct, as in previous example (a).

Rests within a tuplet

Keep separate rests for each division of a tuplet where this clarifies division. It can be clearer not to present rests in their most abbreviated durations:

However, it is best to amalgamate rests within groups of short durations, so that the groups can be read more quickly:

Tuplet beaming

Groups with single beams

Beam each tuplet separately to give the rhythmic groupings maximum clarity:

It is usually best to separate tuplets from other beamed notes, as the rhythms are then much clearer to read:

(To show how a bracket can clarify the extent of a tuplet, see *When to use brackets*, p. 199.)

Groups with inner beams

The outer beam can join together subdivided units as long as the inner beam is divided for each tuplet. Undivided inner beams obscure the rhythm:

Beaming and labelling subdivided tuplets according to accentuation

It is important to separate the innermost beams to reflect the correct subdivision of a tuplet.

When it is the tuplet itself that subdivides, the numeral indicates the division of the whole group (and not the subdivisions). This is how the rhythm is stressed (see bracketed accents), and the beaming should reflect this accentuation (Table 5, first column).

When two groups of tuplets are joined by one beam, either each group takes a separate tuplet numeral (see second column), or the sum of the numerals appears as one centred numeral (third column):

TABLE 5: Beaming and labelling subdivided tuplets according to accentuation

DIFFERENTIATING TRIPLETS FROM SEXTUPLETS

A triplet is always a tripartite division, whereas a sextuplet is two groups each of three notes, a bipartite division (see Table 5, opposite). It is incorrect to beam a triplet without subdividing the beams, as the division would then be unclear:

Group rests according to the correct rhythmic division:

LABELLING A TUPLET OF MIXED NOTE-VALUES

Such subdivided tuplets should use the numeral with the smallest multiple, i.e. the numeral for the division of the whole group, and not the smallest note-value:

(See also *Stating the tuplet ratio in full*, p. 207.)

Tuplets within tuplets

Placing numerals and brackets

Enclose the tuplet numeral for the entire division in a bracket so that it is clear it applies to the whole group. A numeral for a subdivided group requires a bracket only when the numeral is on the notehead side of the group (see *When to use brackets*, p. 199).

Where there is room, place one tuplet indication on either side of the group. The indication for the whole group should go on the stem side:

When all other tuplet indications in a passage are above the stave, place the indication for the whole group above the stave:

When both tuplet indications need to be on the same side of the group, place the indication for the whole tuplet furthest from the group:

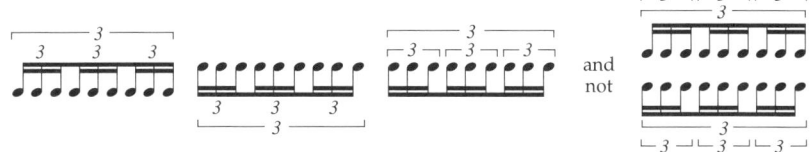

Note-values of triplets

When a triplet subdivides into further triplets, the note-values look slower than their longer standard-division equivalents:

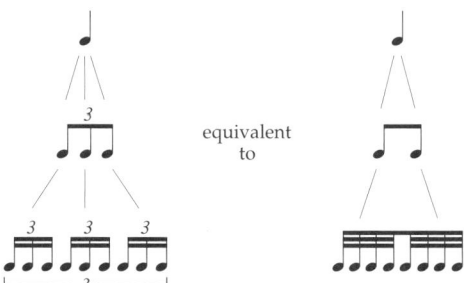

However, when nine notes are in the time of a crotchet, and the tuplet group is to be without internal accentuation, this can be written as follows:

Tuplet repetition

Groups of identical rhythmic patterns may drop the numeral after a bar or two, provided that the rhythmic grouping remains clear:

[musical example in 2/4 with triplet groupings]

However, when there is complex rhythmic alignment in a full score, numerals are best included throughout so that the conductor can see the alignment at a glance.

Tuplets of repeated single notes or chords may be abbreviated:

In both cases, *sim.* may be added for clarity once the numeral is omitted.

(See *Tuplet division (triplets, quintuplets, etc.)*, p. 219.)

8
Repeat Signs

TREMOLOS 219

Principles of repeated-note abbreviation 219

Tremolo definition 220

Single-note tremolos 221

Two-note tremolos 225

REPEAT-BEAT AND REPEAT-BAR ABBREVIATION 230

REPEATED SECTIONS 233

Da Capo and Dal Segno layouts 238

Tremolos

Principles of repeated-note abbreviation

A repeated number of notes can be abbreviated provided that the repeated note-value is a quaver or shorter. The repeated notes are usually a tremolo except for quavers or semiquavers in a slow tempo.

Diagonal lines through a stem indicate the note-value of the repetition. These are the tremolo strokes. Each stroke added to the stem doubles the number of repetitions:

Each stroke is, in effect, a shorthand beam. Deduct one stroke for every beam or tail that is added to the stem:

Tuplet division (triplets, quintuplets, etc.)

Repeated-note abbreviation may indicate repeated tuplets. A numeral represents the divisions of the initial note-value:

triplets   quintuplets   septuplets

The numeral multiplies according to the number of tuplets contained within the note-value:

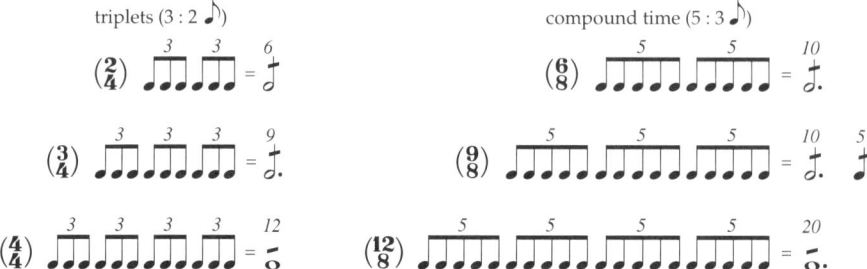

Allocate the appropriate tuplet numeral to each stem, or place it above the stave (if this is where surrounding numerals are positioned):

A tuplet is clearest unabbreviated at its first appearance (see *When to use abbreviation*, p. 223).

TRIPLETS (AND THEIR MULTIPLES) IN SIMPLE TIME

Traditionally, note-values were converted into compound time by adding durations dots:

It is now standard practice to notate the actual value of the initial note, to avoid confusion over duration:

Tremolo definition

Measured tremolo: this is the fast repetition of notes measured exactly in a given tempo. The effect is to create audible rhythmic subdivisions of the written beats (see *Measured tremolos*, p. 224).

Unmeasured tremolo: this is repetition played as fast as possible, without perceptibly defined rhythm (see *Unmeasured tremolos*, p. 224).

The single-note tremolo: this is the rapid re-articulation of a single note or chord, which may be either measured or unmeasured.

The two-note tremolo: this is the rapid alternation (either measured or unmeasured) of two different pitches or chords (see *Two-note tremolos*, p. 225).

Tremolo strokes are used in woodwind and brass writing to indicate flutter-tonguing.

Single-note tremolos

Design of the tremolo stroke

Each stroke is a little thinner than a beam (see *Beams: Design*, p. 17). This is so that the spaces between the strokes are slightly wider than between beams (the spacing of strokes for both is the same). Thus the strokes are less likely to fill in and obscure a rhythm when placed against stave-lines.

The stroke is the width of a notehead, and is centred on the stem.

Strokes should not be too thin or they will be inconspicuous on the stave:

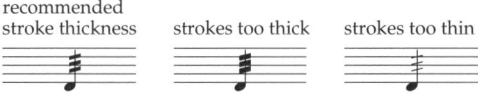

POSITION ON THE STAVE

A tremolo of only one stroke intersects a stave-line:

Two or more strokes must be at least one stave-space clear of a notehead, so as not to obscure it:

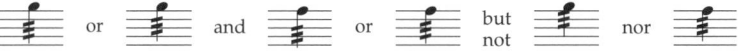

A stem should extend beyond the outermost stroke. It will need to be longer than normal to accommodate three (or more) strokes:

When a tremolo note has a tail or beam, extend a stem if necessary, so that the tremolo strokes are clear of tails and beams. Where there are one or two strokes, it is clearest if they centre on stave-lines:

If tremolo strokes intersect a tail or beam, they will obscure the duration:

Tremolo strokes must stay within the stave so as not to be confused with, nor collide with, a ledger line:

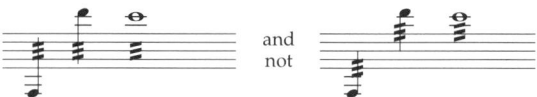

The semibreve has the same width of tremolo stroke as other note values, which means the strokes are slightly shorter than the width of the notehead. Centre the semibreve strokes on the notehead, and place them above or below it according to the notional position of a stem:

On adjacent-note chords, the strokes remain the same width as for single-note repetitions. For semibreves, the tremolo strokes centre on the note that is notionally on the 'correct' side of the stem:

SINGLE-NOTE TREMOLOS 223

ANGLE OF STROKES

Tremolo strokes slant diagonally from bottom left to top right, regardless of stem direction or beam angle:

recommended

In some editions, the slant is slightly steeper than the steepest beam angle. In other editions, beamed groups take strokes of beam thickness (i.e. thicker than the diagonal tremolo strokes), which are placed parallel to the beam; notes without beams have the thinner diagonal strokes (as in bar 2):

acceptable

Repeated articulation

Articulation may be added for repeated-note abbreviation and measured tremolo notes. Centre on the notehead the number of articulation marks appropriate for the number of repetitions:

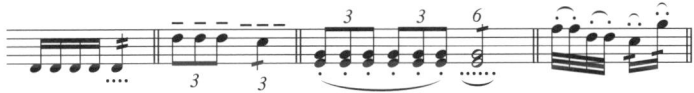

A single accent may be used if it applies to the first note only:

An accent may also be used to indicate the accented first note of an unmeasured tremolo:

When to use abbreviation

With measured tremolo, reserve abbreviation for extended repetition. Isolated figures should be written out in full, as they are much easier to read unabbreviated:

Notate tuplet abbreviations in full at their first appearance, before abbreviating them:

Notate fast, measured repetition in full initially, so that it is not misinterpreted as unmeasured tremolo (see below).

Unmeasured tremolo repetition is always abbreviated.

Measured tremolos

It is sometimes unclear whether a tremolo should be measured or unmeasured because of inadequate specification. The abbreviation 𝄎 defines the unmeasured tremolo so frequently that this notation will be read as unmeasured unless otherwise indicated.

It is therefore advisable to notate the first beat or bar of a measured tremolo in full. (It is then assumed that this same rhythm will apply to subsequent note abbreviations.) For absolute clarity, add the label *non trem.* to the first note-value of abbreviation:

i.e. continuing in the rhythm of the first beat

Unmeasured tremolos

The standard indication is three tremolo strokes. The notation implies that the repetition is too fast to measure in the given tempo, and therefore must be unmeasured. Should it be possible to measure the repeated notes in the given tempo, add a further tremolo stroke to each note.

Since percussionists are able to play very fast tremolos measured where even 𝄎 may be ambiguous, indicate *trem.* over the first note of an unmeasured tremolo passage in a moderate or slow tempo (as in the example below).

After a tremolo passage it is useful to alert the reader to the first non-tremolo note with a *non trem.* indication:

As long as it does not make the rhythm difficult to read, the changes of technique are best clarified with separate beaming:

TIES

Ties may join consecutive unmeasured tremolo notes of the same pitch to discourage any slight accent on a subsequent beat. Dotted ties are sometimes used, since the tie is not literal, but solid ties are visually less complicated to read.

Repeat an accidental over a barline should a dotted tie be used (this is unnecessary with a solid tie):

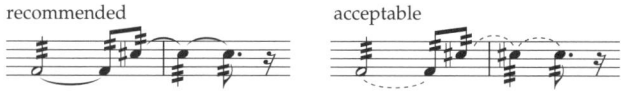

Two-note tremolos

The two-note tremolo is the alternation of two different pitches or chords: it is rapid alternation in an unmeasured tremolo (see *Unmeasured tremolos*, p. 224), and rhythmically precise alternation in a measured tremolo (see *Measured tremolos*, p. 224).

The two-note tremolo is notated with beams of ordinary beam thickness and centred between the stems (or notional stems) of the relevant pitches.

Written note-values

The two-note tremolo is a notational anomaly in that both note-values take the full duration of the tremolo:

Sometimes, in older scores, crotchet tremolos are joined by a quaver beam, but this is incorrect:

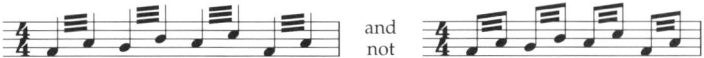

Positioning tremolo beams

Except for minim tremolos, tremolo beams are not attached to stems. Minim tremolos can be beamed in one of three ways:

When beams and stems are separate, position the beams between the stems of the two pitches as if they were joined to the stems. However, the detached beams may move slightly closer to the noteheads than attached ones, so that stems are not forced to be greatly extended (compare the beam positions in the example above).

Both stems must point in the same direction and enclose all the beams. Stems for notes equidistant from the middle stave-line may go in either direction:

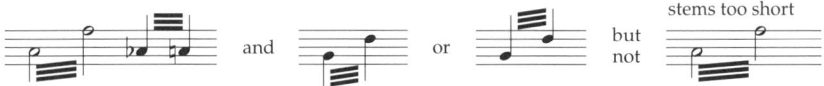

If the interval between the two pitches is an octave or more, it is acceptable to place the beams between the notes (both of which take conventional stem direction). This saves space outside the stave. The beams slant in the direction of the interval:

For semibreves, position the tremolo beams as if the semibreves were stemmed (notional stems are here represented by dotted lines):

It is acceptable to move semibreve beams close to noteheads, to save space outside the stave. This should be avoided if the close proximity of beams and notes or ledger lines is visually confusing:

BETWEEN TWO STAVES

For a braced part on two staves, place tremolo beams for semibreves as if the notes were beamed mid-system (notional stems are represented by dotted lines in the following example). When only one of the beams is attached to both stems (as in bar 3), the tremolo beams go below:

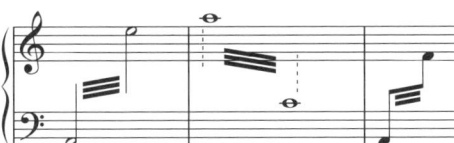

Second-note alignment

Place the second note rhythmically (not visually) exactly halfway through the duration of the tremolo.

The following examples shows vertical alignment with another part in score format:

dotted notes

Length of tremolo beams

Beams stop just short of each stem (or the notional position of the stem on stemless notes). The distance from each stem should be the same. Thus the tremolo beams for two parts on one stave will not align precisely (this is illustrated below by dotted lines):

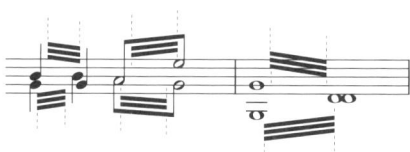

Beams for widely spaced tremolo notes may be uniformly shortened so as not to look ungainly:

Separating each two-note tremolo

It is usually helpful visually to beam individual two-note tremolos separately. Divide tremolos from each other and from non-tremolo notes:

Slurs

Attach a slur to a two-note tremolo only when this is the required articulation. A slur is essential when the second note has no separate articulation.

In wind and string notation, when the tremolo is part of a phrase with no separate articulation, do not add slurs for tremolos as well, as this causes confusion as to whether each tremolo is separately articulated (i.e. tongued or bowed) or not:

(See *Slurs within slurs*, p. 113.)

Tremolos lasting more than single note-values

To tie two-note tremolos (with a solid or dotted tie) is not at all practical. The resulting visual complexity outweighs any apparent clarification of articulation. A slur for the whole figure is recommended to replace the function of the tie, i.e. to prevent rearticulation or accentuation at the beginning of subsequent notes:

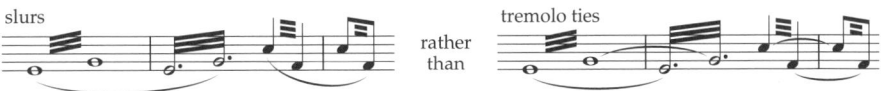

Tremolos between three or more pitches

These are played by repeating the three or more pitches in sequence. All notes take the full value of the tremolo duration. When the tremolo is between three pitches, place each note one third of the way through the tremolo duration, for four notes a quarter of the way through, and so on. Centre the tremolo beams across the middle values. All the notes of a minim tremolo may be beamed together:

Britten adopted this clear and efficient notation in his late works (see, for example, *Death in Venice*).

Harp tremolos have their own notation and so do not need to be written in this way. They are written as single-note tremolo chords, even though each note will be played separately.

(To notate variation in tremolo speed, see *Beamed groups indicating variation in speed*, p. 158; see also *Variation in trill speed*, p. 139.)

Repeat-beat and Repeat-bar Abbreviation

Using abbreviation

In full scores: abbreviation is ideally suited to the repetition of simple material where score-reading will not be unduly hampered by the abbreviation signs. For this reason, these abbreviations are appropriate in entertainment and theatre music. Abbreviation is inappropriate for complex textures, since the abbreviation signs obscure simultaneous events. Therefore, in general, this type of abbreviation is not suited to concert-music scores.

In instrumental parts: except where there is a shortage of space, it is best to fully notate repeated material, so that performers can follow by eye what they are playing. The abbreviation signs given below may, however, be used, especially for extended repetition. Avoid a one-off repeat abbreviation, unless space is very limited, as this interrupts the visual progress of the music on the page. Easily memorable material is the most suitable for abbreviation, since the reader can look onwards with the repeated bars, rather than needing to refer back to the first statement of the material and risking losing the place.

Repeated beats

This notation is appropriate only in instrumental parts of entertainment and theatre music.

A diagonal line of beam thickness, centred in the middle two stave-spaces, indicates repetition of the preceding beamed group. A single diagonal line represents quaver groups, two lines represent semiquaver groups, and three lines represent demisemiquaver groups:

Beat repetition may continue over a change of metre, provided that the written duration of the beat is unchanged:

If the written duration of the beat changes, the repeat should be written out with the new note-values:

Repeated chords

This notation is appropriate for indicating repeated chords with a variety of rhythms (regular, repeated rhythms should use repeated-note abbreviation: see *Principles of repeated-note abbreviation*, p. 219).

For note-values of less than a crotchet, stems alone may indicate repeated chords. The stems should be of identical length to the initial chord. Restate repeated pitches at the start of a new system. In an instrumental part in a fast tempo, this notation may be more helpful than the full notation of every chord, since it is immediately clear where a chord changes. It can also be space-saving:

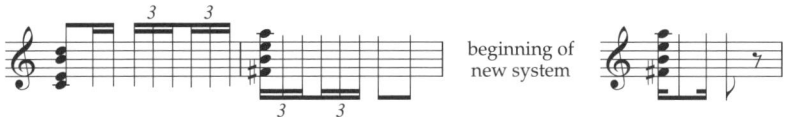

Repeated crotchets: a diagonal line through the middle two stave-spaces may be used in entertainment and theatre music:

Minims are not abbreviated.

Repeated bars

These repeat signs are suitable for use in instrumental parts in all musical genres.

SINGLE-BAR REPEATS

The abbreviation for a repeated bar is a diagonal line of beam thickness, placed in the middle two stave-spaces with a bold dot on either side.

In order to use this abbreviation sign, the content of a bar must be an identical repetition of the previous bar; otherwise, the bar should be notated in full. A bar beginning with a tie or a slur cannot use the single-bar repeat sign:

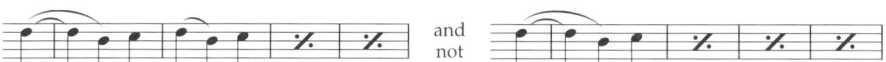

Bars of tied notes alone should be written out in full:

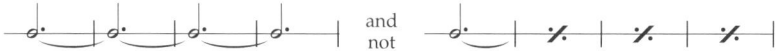

A dynamic indication given in the bar to be repeated will apply to every repeated bar, unless cancelled:

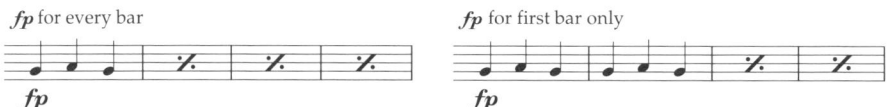

Changes of dynamic during bars of the abbreviation sign are acceptable:

An abbreviation sign cannot be used after a change of metre, nor should it be placed after bars of rests. Notate the music of the repeated bar at the beginning of each system so that it is not necessary to look back to a previous system.

In instrumental parts, bars of repeat signs should be numbered. The first statement of the material (and not the first repeat) is '1' (see following example).

TWO-BAR REPEATS

For the two-bar abbreviation, parallel diagonal lines bisect the barline. The sign is used in the same way as the single-bar repeat. In an instrumental part, number each pair of bars, the first statement being '1'.

Use the two-bar repeat sign very sparingly, ideally only for a self-contained, two-bar figure. Good layout is essential so that the eye skips back to the correct place. Unless preceded by a rest, place the two-bar material at the beginning of a system; thus it will be separated visually from the music that is before it. The initial two bars should never be divided over a system break:

A two-bar repeat should not include whole-bar rests:

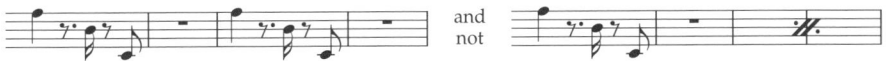

It should not repeat two identical single-bar repeats, nor be combined with single-bar repeat signs:

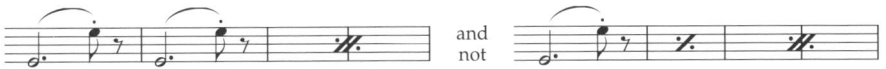

Repeated Sections

Placing repeat barlines

Repeat barlines frame a section to be repeated, except where the repeat is from the beginning of a piece, in which case no initial repeat barline is needed.

Repeat barlines may be placed at any point in the bar. At a conventional barline, they replace it. When the repeat barlines do not coincide with the metrical barline, the value of the beats at each end of the repeat must add up to a whole bar:

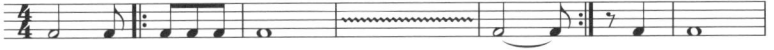

A repeated section that does not coincide with barlines (as above) may instead use first- and second-time endings, to allow repeats to coincide with (and replace) ordinary barlines. The incomplete bar is taken into a first-time bar (see *First- and second-time endings*, p. 236).

Where possible, the beginning of a repeat should coincide with a new system. This makes the section easiest to locate. When a repeated section does not coincide with the barline, incomplete bars may be placed on consecutive systems:

Some editions place a thin double barline at the end of a previous system where a repeat barline starts the next system.

To repeat adjacent sections, use repeat barlines back to back. Either of the following designs may be used:

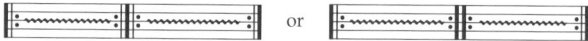

Placing changes of clef, key signature and time signature

When there is a new clef, key signature or time signature at the beginning of a repeated section, place the repeat marks afterwards:

(If the example above were the opening of a piece, the initial repeat barline would be unnecessary.)

When a clef, key signature or time signature changes during a repeated passage, it must be reinstated for the repeat. Create a first-time bar for this information:

After a change in the first-time bar, a reminder in brackets of a continuing clef, key signature or time signature is helpful at the beginning of the second-time bar:

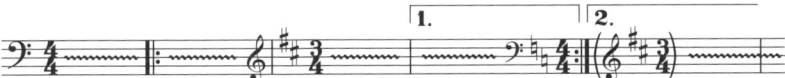

When the change applies to a passage that follows the repeat as well, place the warning clef, key signature or time signature at the end of the repeated section:

CHANGES AFTER A REPEAT

A change that affects the music only after a repeat goes after the repeat barline:

It is useful to add reminder accidentals and dynamics in brackets for the performer returning to the beginning of a repeat:

Variation in repeat sections

When there is any variation between repeats, a repeated section should be written out in full, with the exception of the following.

When a player is silent for some of the bars within one repeat, or for a whole repeat, state this verbally over the stave, e.g. *play 1st/2nd time only* or *1st/2nd time tacet*:

Alternatively, when there is a very small difference, such as a single note to be played once only, this may be written as a cue note with a whole-bar rest above or beneath. Add a verbal instruction such as *1st/2nd time only*.

Dynamics or tempo changes that differ for a repeat are placed in brackets after first-time indications:

When instructions become complicated, a repeated passage is clearest written out in full.

First- and second-time endings

These may be indicated in English or Italian: *first time* or *prima volta*; *second time* or *seconda volta*; and *final time* or *ultima volta*.

Any variation at all between repeat endings, however small (e.g. a pause on the final ending), requires separate endings in the form of first- and second-time bars.

Brackets above the system enclose the relevant bars for each repeat. The number of repeats is given within each bracket (use numerals the size and appearance of time-signatures):

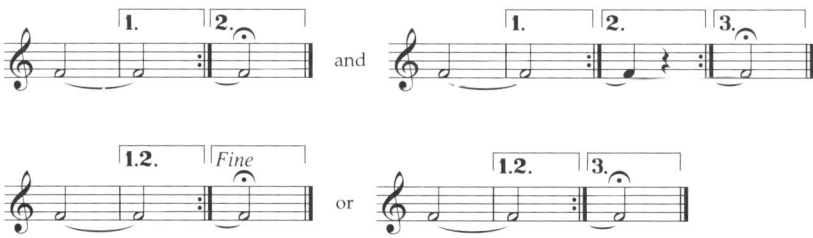

Place brackets in the same position as tempi: in an orchestral score, this is above the top stave and also above the strings. Tempo indications or rehearsal marks that coincide with first- and second-time bars may be placed above or within the bracket, according to available space.

REPEATED SECTIONS 237

SEPARATE ENDING SECTIONS OF MORE THAN A BAR'S LENGTH

Enclose the first-time bars (and any further repeated sections before the final-time repeat) in a bracket. Across a system break the first-time bracket is open-ended. The final section bracket extends for usually one bar only (or two short bars) and remains open-ended:

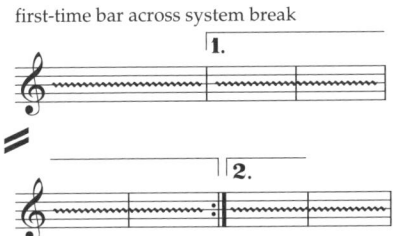

At the end of a piece, to look more final, run a second-time bar to the end (provided it is shorter than a whole system) and close it parallel to the final double barline.

BAR NUMBERS

Some editions duplicate first- and second-time bar numbers as shown below. If this is the case, the second-time bracket must enclose the bars that have the duplicate numbers (this will be equal to the number of first-time bars). It is also useful to number each bar, for clarity:

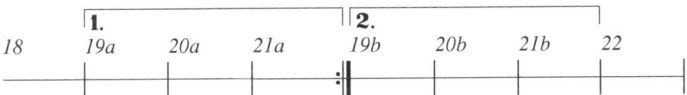

In ensemble music, it is best to number consecutively through separate endings, to avoid confusion when counting bars during rehearsal. For clarity, indicate the numbers of the first-time bars and the first second-time bar:

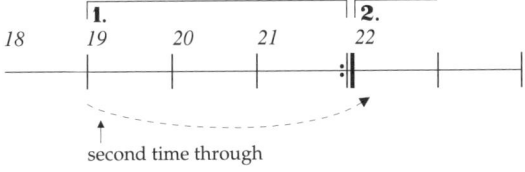

Da Capo and Dal Segno layouts

Section repetition using an accepted familiar layout, such as verse form in vocal music, and the minuet (or scherzo) and trio in instrumental music, requires the clear demarcation only of sections (or verses) that are to be repeated.

Where a piece involves anything other than straight repetition, the following Italian terms signpost the reader through repeated sections, replacing repeat signs:

Da Capo (abbrev. *D.C.*) means '[repeat] from the beginning'.

Dal Segno (abbrev. *D.S.*) means '[repeat] from the sign (marked 𝄋)'.

(In the examples below, the word *Segno* may be replaced or followed by 𝄋.)

Add the phrase *al Fine* ('to the end') to the above terms when the end of the piece (indicated *Fine*) is not at the written end of the music.

Da Capo al Fine (also marked only as *Da Capo*) means 'from the beginning to the end' (i.e. as far as the bar marked *Fine*):

Dal Segno al Fine (often marked only as *Dal Segno*) means 'from the sign to the end' (i.e. to *Fine*):

LAYOUT WITH A CODA

The traditional coda sign is ⊕. When skipping to a final section or coda after a repeated section (as described above), the point of departure for the final section is marked ⊕.

Layout is set out as follows.

D.C. al ⊕ *e poi la Coda* (also abbreviated to *D.C. al Coda* or *D.C. al* ⊕) means 'from the beginning to the sign and then skip to the coda':

For visual clarity, the coda sign may be placed both at the point of departure for the coda and at its start (see last example, below).

Dal Segno 𝄋 al Segno ⊕ e poi la Coda (also abbreviated to *D.S. al Coda* or *D.S. al ⊕*) means 'repeat from the sign 𝄋 to the sign ⊕ and then skip to the coda'. It is important to include both signs in the instruction, to clarify which is which:

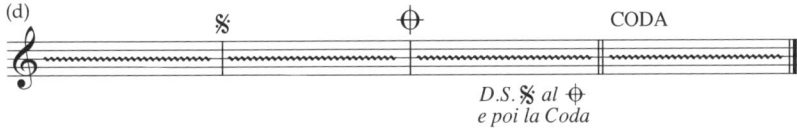

Be aware that the layout in the example above may be difficult to negotiate without getting lost, especially if it involves page-turns between the different sections. Rehearsal time may be used up rehearsing the geography of the piece rather than the music. In such cases, notate all or some of the repeated sections in full, so as not to risk jeopardizing a secure performance.

When the reader must skip a section to a coda, make its location conspicuous:

- Mark it with a thin double barline, the label *Coda* or ⊕, or even use all three for added clarity (see following example)
- When the coda begins on a new system, indent the system. Place the coda label or sign above the system or, if convenient, in the indented margin of an instrumental part
- When the coda begins mid-system, where there is room, blank out a preceding section of stave and place the coda label or sign there (in a single-stave part) or above the stave (in a score or braced part):

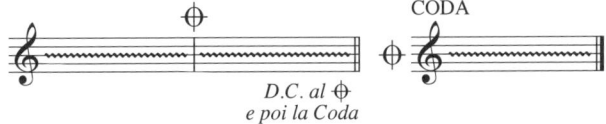

Note that clef and key signature must be reinstated after the stave break. In a score, restate margin brackets as well; in a braced part, restate the curly brace.

POSITIONING THE SIGNS

The sign 𝄋 should always signal a point from which to repeat. The coda sign ⊕ indicates a point from which to skip ahead.

The signs 𝄋 and ⊕ go above the stave (or top stave of a system), centred over the barline.

Da Capo, *Dal Segno* and *Fine* instructions are written in a conspicuous font, to differentiate them from surrounding text: in a vocal score or orchestral part this might be italic, otherwise bold. Place them above the top stave of a vocal score; below the stave of a single-line part; below the bottom stave of a score or braced part.

DOUBLE BARLINES

No repeat barlines (‖: :‖) are used unless there are internal repeats within sections.

A thin double barline, rather than a final double barline, marks the written end of the music when this is not the end of the piece (see examples (a) and (b), p. 238).

Only the *Fine* bar, the actual end of the piece, takes a final double barline. This is regardless of whether the *Fine* is a whole or an incomplete bar. A thin double barline is used for repetition and departure points mid-bar (see (b), p. 238). Otherwise, thin double barlines are not used at repetition and departure points that occur on barlines (see examples (c) and (d), p. 239), unless these coincide with a new music section.

POSITIONING REPEAT SECTIONS

It is helpful if sections to be returned to or skipped to can begin on a new system. This visually demarcates them.

Ideally, a *Fine* bar in the written middle of the piece should be placed at the end of a system.

BAR NUMBERS

Numbering should run consecutively through all written sections. Thus a repeated section will not have independent numbering. A section involving skipping a passage (e.g. to a coda) will have a corresponding skip in bar numbers.

Appendix

Notes, Keys and Symbols: International Terms

242 APPENDIX: INTERNATIONAL TERMS

	ENGLISH	ITALIAN	FRENCH	GERMAN
	C	do	ut/do	C
	D	re	ré	D
	E	mi	mi	E
	F	fa	fa	F
	G	sol	sol	G
	A	la	la	A
	B	si	si	H
	B♭			B
	major	maggiore	majeur	Dur
	minor	minore	mineur	Moll
♯	sharp	diesis	dièse	Kreuz: suffix -is*
♭	flat	bemolle	bémol	Be: suffix -es*
×	double-sharp	doppio diesis	double-dièse	Doppel-Kreuz: suffix -isis*
♭♭	double-flat	doppio bemolle	double-bémol	Doppel-Be: suffix -eses*
♮	natural	bequadro	bécarre	Auflösungszeichen
▷◁ or ◁▷ or ‖	breve *double whole-note*⁵	breve	carrée/brève/ double-ronde	Brevis
o	semibreve *whole-note*⁵	semibreve	ronde	ganze Note

APPENDIX: INTERNATIONAL TERMS

minim / *half-note*[§]	minima/bianca	blanche	halbe Note
crotchet / *quarter-note*[§]	semiminima/nera	noire	Viertelnote
quaver / *eighth-note*[§]	croma	croche	Achtelnote
semiquaver / *sixteenth-note*[§]	semicroma	double-croche	Sechzehntelnote
demisemiquaver / *thirty-second note*[§]	biscroma	triple-croche	Zweiunddreißigstelnote
hemidemisemiquaver / *sixty-fourth note*[§]	semibiscroma	quadruple-croche	Vierundsechzigstelnote

[§] *American usage is shown in italic type.*

* Small irregularities exist in the German; keys are set out in full below.

♯	♭	𝄪	♭♭
Cis	Ces	Cisis	Ceses
Dis	Des	Disis	Deses
Eis	Es	Eisis	Eses
Fis	Fes	Fisis	Feses
Gis	Ges	Gisis	Geses
Ais	As	Aisis	Asas
His	B	Hisis	Heses

Further Reading

Below is a highly selective list of further reading. For a comprehensive bibliography of works on notation, see *The New Grove Dictionary of Music and Musicians*, article on *Notation*, vol. 13. Books on individual instruments are referenced in the text, where relevant. The *New Instrumental Series* (California University Press) includes useful books on the contemporary flute, clarinet, trombone, harp, guitar and double bass. Several titles are out of print but may be found in libraries or online.

Music engraving and notation

Cole, Hugo, *Sounds and Signs: Aspects of Musical Notation* (Oxford University Press, 1974)
Gerou, Tom, and Linda Lusk, *Essential Dictionary of Music Notation* (Alfred Publishing Company, 1996)
Gould, Elaine, *Behind Bars: The Definitive Guide to Music Notation* (Faber Music, 2011)
Homewood, Susan, and Colin Matthews, *The Essentials of Music Copying* (Music Publishers' Association, 1990)
Rastall, Richard, *The Notation of Western Music: An Introduction* (Travis & Emery, 2nd rev. edn, 2008)
Ross, Ted, *The Art of Music Engraving and Processing* (Hansen Books, 3rd edn, 1987)
Sadie, Stanley, and John Tyrrell (eds), *The New Grove Dictionary of Music and Musicians*, 29 vols (Oxford University Press, 2nd edn, 2001) particularly articles on *Aleatory* and *Notation*
Stone, Kurt, *Music Notation in the Twentieth Century: A Practical Guidebook* (W. W. Norton, 1980)

Orchestration

Adler, Samuel, *The Study of Orchestration* (W. W. Norton, 3rd edn, 2002)
Blatter, Alfred, *Instrumentation and Orchestration* (Wadsworth, 2nd rev. edn, 1997)
Del Mar, Norman, *Anatomy of the Orchestra* (Faber and Faber, 1981, re-issued 2009)
Runswick, Daryl, *Rock, Jazz and Pop Arranging* (Faber Music, 1992)

Text editing

New Hart's Rules: The Handbook of Style for Writers and Editors
  (Oxford University Press, 2005)

Copyright Acknowledgements

Birtwistle, Harrison: *Secret Theatre*
© Copyright 1991 by Universal Edition (London) Ltd, London/UE17917
Reproduced by permission. All rights reserved

Bliss, Arthur: Quintet for Oboe and Strings
© Copyright Oxford University Press, 1928
Reproduced by permission of Oxford University Press. All rights reserved

Xenakis, Iannis: *Medea-senecae*
Property of Éditions Salabert SA, Paris
© Editions Salabert, 1970
Reproduced by permission of G. Ricordi & Co. (London) Ltd

Index

Where there are multiple page references, main entries are indicated in **bold** type. Page numbers in *italic* type indicate relevant music examples or tables.

ACCENTS 114–22
ACCIDENTALS 77–91
  altered unisons 50–52, 90–91
  atonal context 82, 85–7
  barlines, after 80–81
  brackets 80, 83
  cancellation **79–82**, 84–5, 86–7, 95
  cautionary 82–3, 235
  chords 87–91
  clef change 78–9
  conventions 83, **86–7**
  courtesy 82–3, 235
  design 77–8, 125
  double flat/sharp 77–8, 81, 85
  double-stemmed writing 80, 90–91
  editorial practice 83, 86–7
  enharmonic-spelling change 85
  grace notes 78, 84, 130
  horizontal spacing **42–3**, 78, 87
  microtones 94–8
    see also microtones
  music without barlines 87
  octave change 78–9, 82
  ornaments 84–5
  reminder 82–3, 235
  shared stave 79–80
  stave change 79
  system break, across 80
  tied notes 80–81
AL FINE, *see* repeated sections
AL NIENTE 108
ALTO CLEF 6, 7
APPOGGIATURA 125
ARPEGGIATED CHORDS 131–4
ARROW CONVENTIONS
  arpeggiated chords **131**, 132
  microtones 94–7
  strum 131
  tempo change 184–5
  tempo equation 186–7
  vibrato change 147
ARTICULATION MARKS 109–22
  accents 114–22
  design 116

  glissando 146
  grace notes 129–30
  intensity (e.g. *sfz*) 115
  marcato 115
  placing 117–22
  repeated-note abbreviation 223
  repetition 116
  shared stave 117–18
  staccatissimo wedge 115, 116–22
  staccato 115, 116–22
  stress symbols 115, 171
  tenuto 115, 116–22
  ties 62
AUGMENTATION DOT, *see* dotted notes

BAR
  barring principles 151
  numbers, repeated sections 237, 240
  numbering for counting 232–3
BARLINE 38–9
  broken 103
  dotted 165, **178–80**
  double **39**, 92, 152, 234, 240
  final 39, 240
  non-coinciding 171, 175–7
  pauses 187
  placing 41, 175–6
  polymetre 174–7
  repeat 39, 183, **233–5**, 240
  systemic 38
  see also repeated sections
BASS CLEF 5
BEAM (design/placing) **17–26**, 35–6, 68
  angled 17, 19–24
  braced-part tremolo 227
  direction 22–4
  double-stemmed (single stave) 26
  fractional 17
  grace notes 125–7
  ledger-line notes 19, 21
  stem direction 24–6
  stem length 15, 18–19, 21, 68
  tremolos 219–29

BEAMING (use of beams) **153–8**, 169–70
  across rests 164–6
  fanned 140, 158
  fractional 157–8, 165
  metres of variable stress 178
  tuplets, grouping 200, 211–13
BEAT STRESS, see cross rhythm; metre
BRACED PART, see harp; keyboard
BRACKETS, square
  editorial accidentals 83
  horizontal
    cross rhythm 171
    note clusters 52
    repeated sections 236–7
  vertical
    non-arpeggiated chords 132
BRASS WRITING, see wind (woodwind and brass) writing
BREVE (notehead) 10

C CLEF 6
CAESURA 187
CHOIR, see choral writing
CHORAL WRITING
  accidentals 79, 83
  dynamics 101, 102
  pauses 189
CHORDS 47–54
  accidentals 87–90
  adjacent-note 27, **48–52**, 55–8, 63, 66, 67, 114, 222
  altered-unison 50–52, 58
  arpeggiation 131–4
  articulation marks to 119
  dotted 55–8
  glissando 143–4
  grace notes to 130
  moving parts 70–71
  note clusters 51–2, 58, 143
  repeat abbreviation 231
  slurred 114
  unison-note **50**, 58–60, 69–70
  see also double-stemmed writing
CHORUS, see choral writing
CLEFS 5–9
  alto 6, 7
  alto trombone 7
  baritone (voice) 6
  bass 5
  bassoon 7
  C 6
  cautionary 235
  cello 7
  change **7–9**, 32, 39, 78–9, 234–5
  glissando, change during 142
  horizontal spacing 6, 41–3
  key-signature change 93
  mezzo-soprano 6
  octave-transposing 32
  percussion 6
  piccolo 32
  soprano clef 6
  tenor 6, 7, 91
  treble 5
  viola 7, 9
CLUSTER, see note cluster
CODA SIGN 238–40
COLL'OTTAVA 32
COMMA 187
COMPOUND TIME
  beaming **154**, 155, 157, 164
  long notes, dividing 167–9
  rests, grouping 160–61, 163–4
  simple time, and 172–4
CONDUCTOR BEATS 176–7, 179
CRESCENDO 101, **103–8**
  see also hairpins
CROSS RHYTHM 171–2
  syncopation 170–71
  see also polymetre
CROTCHET 9–10
  repeat abbreviation 231
COUNTERPOINT 36–7
CUE
  rhythmic 172, 176–7
  symbols, size 125

DA CAPO 238–40
DAL SEGNO 238–40
DAMPING 72–3
DECRESCENDO, see diminuendo
DENOMINATOR 151–2, 180–82
  as notehead 182
  see also time signatures
DIMINUENDO 101, **103–7**
  al niente 108
  see also hairpins
DOTTED NOTES 54–60
  abbreviated triplets 220
  compound-time duplets 205–7
  octave extension line, and 30
  ties, and 63–4, 70
DOUBLE BASS
  clefs 7, 32
  tuning peg, release 13
DOUBLE-STEMMED (TWO-PART) WRITING 52–4, 56–8
  accidentals 79–80, 90–91

adjacent notes 49–50, 53, 54, 56–8, 90–91
articulation marks 117–18
chords 47–50, 57, 58
dotted notes 56–60
dynamics 101–3
grace notes 126, 127, 128, 129
ledger lines 27
overlapping parts 27, **53–4**, 56–8, 67–8, 91, 228
pauses 188, 189
rests, position 35, **36–7**
slurs 111
stem lengths 14, 16
ties, direction 67–8, 199
trills 135–6
unison notes 52–3, 58–60, 69–70, 91
DURATION DOT, *see* dotted notes
DYNAMICS 101–9
   change 106–8, 132–3
   grace notes 130–31
   interim 106–7
   position **101–3**, 105, 110, 132–3, 135
   repetition 108–9
   size 101
   trills, for 135
   see also hairpins; *subito*

ENHARMONIC SPELLING, *see* note-spelling
ENSEMBLE SCORE, *see* full score
ENTERTAINMENT MUSIC 7, 230–33

FALSETTO 11
FERMATA, *see* pause mark
FINE 238, 240
FIRST- AND SECOND-TIME ENDINGS 236–7
FRENCH CONVENTIONS
   adjacent-note chords 49
   key signature, change of 92
   octave signs 28
   open ties 72
FULL SCORE
   accidental conventions 79–80
   barlines 38
   clefs 9, 32
   co-ordination 151, 177–8
   dynamics 101–2
   octave signs 33
   pauses 190
   polymetre 174–6
   poly-tempo 177–8
   slurs, shortening 112
   tempo indications 182–3
   time-signature placing 152
   see also double-stemmed (two-part) writing; vertical alignment

GLISSANDO 140–46
   articulation, and 146
   cancellation 141
   chromatic-scale 140
   clef changes 142
   duration 145–6
   finishing-note articulation 144
   interim pitches 144–5
   microtonal 140
   note clusters 143–4
   parallel-chord 143
   speed 143
   unspecified pitch 13, **142–3**
G.P. (general pause) 190
   vuota 190
GRACE NOTES 43, **125–31**, 138
   accidentals 78, 84, 130
   articulation 129–30
   beat, on/before 127, 128–9
   dynamics, placing 130–31
   ledger lines 26, 126, 129
   stem direction **126–7**, 129
   tails 125–6
   tremolos, and 127
   trills, and 127, 138, 139
   vertical alignment 127–9, 159
GRAPHIC NOTATION
   glissando contour 146
   vibrato, changes in 147

HAIRPINS 103–8
   arpeggiated chords 132–3
HARMONICS
   diamond-shaped noteheads 11
HARP WRITING
   accidentals 79, 86
   arpeggiation 131–4
   beam, common 26, 227
   dynamics, placing 101, *105*
   glissando 140, 143
   key signatures 93
   ledger lines 32–4
   note-spelling 93
   octave signs 33–4
   octave-transposing clefs 32
   tremolos 227–8, 229
HIGHEST NOTE 12–13, 143

INTERLOCKING STEMS, *see* part crossing
IRREGULAR NOTE DIVISION, *see* tuplets

KEY SIGNATURES 91–4
   cautionary 235
   key change 39, **92–3**

key signatures, contd
   non-tonal/polytonal music 93–4
   order of accidentals 91, 92
   ornaments 85
   placing 41–3, 234–5
KEYBOARD WRITING
   accidentals 79, 86
   arpeggiation 131–4
   beam, common 26, 227
   double-stemmed unisons 59
   dynamics, placing 101, *105*
   glissando 140, 143–4
   ledger lines 32–4
   notes sustained in pedal 73
   octave signs 32–4
   octave-transposing clefs 32
   two-stave tremolo 227–8
   see also piano writing

LAISSEZ VIBRER 72–3
   l.v. sempre 72
   piano 73
   rests 72–3
LASCIAR VIBRARE, *see laissez vibrer*
LAYOUT, GENERAL PRINCIPLES
   symbols, spacing (horizontal) 39–43
   see also full score; spacing (horizontal); vertical alignment
LEDGER LINES AND NOTES 7, **26–7**, **32–4**, 142
   articulation marks 120–21
   beam, placing 19, 21
   dotted notes 55
   grace notes 26, 126, 129
   keyboard writing 33
   minimizing 33
   overlapping parts 27
   performance material 7, 33
   rests, and 36, 37
   stem length **14–16**, 18–19, 21, 26, 27
   string writing 33
   tails, and 16
   ties, and 66, 68
   tremolo strokes, and 222
   woodwind writing 33
LIGATURE, *see* beam
LOCO 34
LOWEST NOTE 12–13, 143
LUNGA 187
L.V., *see laissez vibrer*

MARCATO 115
METRE 151, **153–82**
   alternating time signatures 179–80
   beaming 153–8
   concurrent, *see* polymetre
   double barline 39, 152

   grouping to contradict 169, 170–72
   interchanging simple/compound time 172–4
   relationship between metres 172–3
   see also metric equation
   rests, grouping 160–64, 178, 179
   unconventional 180–82
   variable bar division 178–9
   see also bar; beaming; cross rhythm; polymetre; syncopation; tempo equation
METRIC EQUATION
   alternating metres *179*
   constant beat 173, *231*
   division of beat constant 172
   polymetre 176
   see also tempo equation
METRIC MODULATION, *see* tempo equation
METRONOME MARKINGS 183–5
MICROTONES 94–8
   glissando 140
   quarter-tones 94–6, 97
   third-tones 97
   vibrato 146
MINIM 10
MORDENT 84
MULTIPLE RESTS 190

NIENTE 108
NON ARPEGGIANDO 132
NON TREM. 224–5
NON VIB. 147
NOTE CLUSTER 51–2
   glissando 143–4
NOTE-SPELLING (ENHARMONICS) 81, **85**
   harp 93
   microtones 95
NOTE-SPACING, *see* rhythmic spacing
NOTEHEADS 9–13
   adjacent 53–4, 56–8, 90–91
   see also chords: adjacent-note
   crossed 11–12
   denominator as 182
   diamond-shaped 11–12
   displacement 48–54
   dots, placing 54–60
   double (unisons) 50–52
   grace notes 125, 129
   size 10
   spacing 39–43, 158
   triangular 12–13, 143
   see also note cluster; unisons; vertical alignment

OCTAVE
   accidentals 78–9, 82

signs 28–34
　with other symbols 28–9, 101, *102*
　with the octave/*col 8* 32
OCTAVE-TRANSPOSING CLEFS 32
OPEN TIES 72–3
ORNAMENT 84–5
　see also trill
OTTAVA ALTA 28
OTTAVA BASSA 28
OTTAVA SOPRA 28
OVERLAPPING PARTS, see part crossing

PART, INSTRUMENTAL
　extraction from score shared stave
　　accidentals 79
　multiple rests 190
　repeat-bar abbreviation 30, 230, 231–2
　repeat-beat abbreviation 230–32
　repeat-chord abbreviation 231
　time-signature placing 152
　see also entertainment music; performance material
PART CROSSING (overlapping parts) 27, **53–4**, 56–8, 67–8, 91
PART EXTRACTION, see performance material
PAUSE MARK 187–90
　unmeasured bars 190
PERCUSSION WRITING
　instruments of indefinite pitch 5, 129
　　clefs 6
　　noteheads 12
　　staves 5, 6
　notes sustained in pedal 73
　unmeasured tremolo (roll) 224
PERFORMANCE MATERIAL
　accidentals 79–82
　clef changes 7, 9
　dynamics 105, 108–9
　ledger lines 7, **33**
　octave signs 33
　tuplet indications 197–9
　see also part, instrumental
PHRASE MARKS 109
　see also slur
PIANO WRITING
　laissez vibrer 73
　ledger lines 32–4
　pedal markings 29, 73
　silently depressed keys 11
　see also keyboard writing
PITCH
　alteration, see accidentals; microtones
　approximate 5, 12
　extreme, unspecifiable 12–13, 143
　indefinite 5, 6, 12

　non-specific 5, 142–3
　retaining pitch contour 7, 8, 33–4
　　glissando 142–3
　　vibrato 147
POLYMETRE 174–8
　coinciding barlines 174–5
　non-coinciding barlines 171, **175–7**
　rhythmic relationship grid 176–7
　see also cross rhythm
POLY-TEMPO 177–8
PORTAMENTO 140
PROPORTIONAL SPACING (TIME–SPACE NOTATION) 39

QUARTER-TONES, see microtones
QUAVER 15–16
　beaming 153–5, 156–7
　tail design 15–16

REPEAT-BAR ABBREVIATION 30, **230**, 231–3
REPEAT-BEAT ABBREVIATION 230–32
REPEATED-NOTE ABBREVIATION, see tremolo; tuplets: repetition
REPEATED CHORDS 231
REPEATED SECTIONS 233–40
　al fine 238
　da capo 238–40
　dal segno 238–40
　incomplete bars 233–4
　octave extension line 30–31
　variation within section 235–7
　see also barlines: repeat
REST SYMBOLS 34–8
　breve **34–5**, 38, 160
　crotchet 35–8
　dotted 38
　dynamics, and 104, 106–7
　ledger lines, and 36, 37
　minim 34–7
　multiple 190
　octave extension line, and 31
　quaver 35–8
　semibreve **34–8**, 159–60
　single-line stave 38
　vertical alignment 159–60
　vertical displacement 35–7
　whole-bar rests 159–60
RESTS: GROUPING 160–64
　beams across rests 164–6
　compound-time 163–4
　dotted 161–3
　metre, and **160–64**, 178, 179
　multiple 190
　simple-time 162–3
　whole-bar 159–60

RESTS: USE
   laissez vibrer 72–3
   shared stave 36–7
   strict counterpoint 36–7
RHYTHMIC SPACING, *see* spacing (horizontal)
RINFORZANDO/RINFORZATO 115

SCORE LAYOUT, *see* full score
SEGNO (symbol) 238–40
SEMIBREVE 10, 180
   see also stemless note
SEMIQUAVER 16, 154, 156–7
SFORZANDO/SFORZATO 115
SILENT BARS, *see* G.P.; *tacet*
SIMILE (SIM.) 116, 215
SIMPLE TIME 160–63, 167–9, 172–4
SLIDE (pitch), *see* glissando; portamento
SLUR **109–14**, 117, 121–2
   divided 112
   double-stemmed writing 117–18
   grace notes 129–30
   legato 113
   reverberation, *see laissez vibrer*
   slurs within slurs 113
   strings 109, 113, 228
   syllabic slur 109
   tie: distinction **60–61**, 65, 68, 71, 81, 109, 112, 122
   tremolos, two-note 228
   tuplets 102, 197–8
   vocal writing 109
   wind 109, 113
SPACING (horizontal) **39–43**, 158
   barlines 41, 175–6
   rests 159–60
   see also vertical alignment
SPOKEN TEXT 12
STACCATISSIMO 115
STACCATO 115, 116–22
STAVE **5**, 6
   indentation 239
STAVE SHARING, *see* double-stemmed writing
STAVE-SPACE **5**, 54–60, 61, 63, 66
STEM 13–15
   grace note, double-stemmed 129
   overlapping intervals 53–4, 56–8, 67–8
   pronged 50–51, 58
   spacing relative to barline 43
   without notehead
      glissando 145–6
      repeat-chord abbreviation 231
   see also double-stemmed writing; string writing
STEM DIRECTION 13–14
   beamed groups 24–6

   chords 47–8
   down-stem convention **13–14**, 25, 47–8
   grace notes 126–7, 129
   tremolos, two-note 226
   up-stem convention (vocal) 14
STEM LENGTH 14–15
   beams 15, **18–19**, 21, 26, 36
   chords 15
   double-stemmed writing 14
   grace notes 125–6
   ledger-line notes **14–15**, 19, 21, 26
   tails, and **15–16**, 55, 61
   tremolos, and 222, 226, 227–8
STEMLESS NOTE 10, 12
   adjacent-note chords 50, 52, 222
   articulation marks 119
   displaced note 50, 52, 58–60
   dotted 58–9
   glissando finishing note 144
   slurs, and 110
   tied 64, 69
   tremolos 222, 226–8, 229
   trilling note 138–9
   two-part writing 52, 54, 69
   unisons **52**, 59, 69
STEMLET 165–6
STRESS, *see* articulation marks
STRING WRITING (bowed instruments)
   de-tuning 13
   glissando 140, 143
   harmonics 11
   ledger lines 33
   multiple-stopping 47
   octave signs 33
   pizzicato chords 131, 143
   portamento 140
   slurs 109, 113, 228
   stem conventions 47
   tremolos, two-note 228
SUBITO 107–8, 185
SYNCOPATION 170–71
   cross rhythm 171–2
SYSTEMIC BARLINE 38
SYLLABIC SLUR 109

TACET
   repetition, in 235
   staves 178, 190
TEMPO EQUATION 166–9, 180–81, 183, **185–7**
TEMPO INDICATIONS 182–5
TEMPO PRIMO/SECONDO 184
TENOR CLEF 6, 7, 91
TENUTO 115, 116–22, 188

INDEX 255

TEXT, *see* vocal writing
THEATRE MUSIC, *see* entertainment music
THIRD-TONES, *see* microtones
TIES 60–73
    accidentals, and 71, 80
    adjacent-note chords 63, 66
    breaking 68
    chords, and 61–6, 70–71
    clef change, and 9
    design 60–64
    direction **64–71**, 133–4
    division of beat 166–9, 170–71
    dotted 225
    open (sustained notes) 72–3
        note sustained in pedal 73
    overlapping parts 67–8
    system break, across 65, 80
    tremolos, and 225, 229
    trills, and 139
    unisons 69–70
TIME SIGNATURES 151–2
    alternating 172–4, 179–80
    barline, thin double 39, 152
    cautionary 235
    change over system break 39, 152
    combined metres 179–80
    concurrent 173, 174–7
    denominators 151–2, 180–82
    new movement/section, and 152
    placing 41–2
    repeated section 234–5
    unconventional 180–82
    variable bar division 178–9
TRANSPOSITION
    see octave-transposing clefs
TREBLE CLEF 5
TREMOLO 219–29
    braced part 227–8
    cancellation 224–5
    duration 229
    fanned beams 140
    grace notes, and 127
    measured 220, 223–4
    pause marks, placing 188
    percussion 224
    repeated-note abbreviation **219–20**, 223, 224
    single-note 221–5
    speed, variation in 140
    stroke design 221–3
    ties 225
    trill, distinction 134–5, 139–40
    two-note 221, **225–9**
        string writing 228
        wind writing 228

    unmeasured 221, **224–5**
TRILL 134–40
    continuous 137
    discontinuous 137
    double 135–6
    grace notes, and 127, 138, 139
    octave extension line 30
    re-articulation indicators 136–7
    speed, variation in 139–40
    stem conventions 135
    system break, across **137**, 139
    tremolo, distinction 134–5, 139–40
    trilling note 138–9
TRILL LINE 131, **136–7**, 139
    glissando, as 140, 146
TROMBONE
    clefs 7
    glissando 140
TUPLETS 193–215
    beam grouping 211–13
    brackets 194–200
    note division 210–11
    note-values 203–7
    numerals 193–4
    repetition 215, **219–20**, 223, 224
    rests 166, 195, 199–200, **211**, 213
    rhythmic alignment 200–202
    sextuplets 212–13
    triplet subdivision 203, 212–14
    tuplets within tuplets 213–14
TURN (ORNAMENT) 84
TWO-PART WRITING, *see* double-stemmed writing

UNACCENTED NOTE 115
UNISONS 50–53
    altered 50–52, 58, 69, 91
    articulation, and 119
    dotted-note 58–60
    tied 69–70
    see also chords

VERTICAL ALIGNMENT
    displaced notes 49–53
    grace notes 127–8, 159
    polymetre 174–6
    poly-tempo 177–8
    rests 159–60
    tempo indications 182–3
    tuplets 200–202
    two-note tremolos 227, 229
    see also chords; full score
VIBRAPHONE
    pedal indications 73
VIBRATO 146–7

VOCAL WRITING
    cautionary accidentals 83
    dynamics 101, 102
    glissando 140
    note-spelling 85
    portamento 140
    single-line stave 5
    spoken text 12
    styles 12
    syllabic slurs 109
    technical instructions 101
    up-stem convention 14
    see also choral writing

VOICE-LEADING, *see* part crossing
VUOTA, *see* G.P.

WEDGE
    articulation **115**, 116–18, 120–22
    dynamic 103–8
WIND MUSIC (woodwind and brass writing)
    articulation 109, 113, 228
    glissando 140, 146
    ledger lines 33
    octave signs 33
    octave-transposing instruments/clefs 32
    tremolos, two-note 228